What People A This Book!

"Some people are lucky enough to go from college to professional sports. I was one of those people. But if you're like most college students you need something to help you make it in the Real World. Jim Malinchak has given you the tool to unlock some of those closed doors in society. This book is not only a MUST read for college students but it could be the KEY TO YOUR SUCCESS."

-Joe Theismann
Former World Champion Quarterback (Washington Redskins)
& Current ESPN Football Analyst

"THESE TECHNIQUES WORK! James Malinchak covers every nook and cranny. I got my dream job on the first resume I sent out. This book is a MUST for any person entering the job market."

-Jeff Hackett
Recent Graduate, California State University-Northridge

"The most powerful book you'll ever read! James Malinchak gives straight forward information to help you get hired. This will be the absolute best decision you make in your job search. READ THIS BOOK!"

-Brad Kehm
Recent Graduate & 1994-95 National Champion
General Motors Internship Challenge

"When I graduated from college I didn't know where to begin. But by using the techniques in this book I not only landed the job I desired but I also landed it in the city where I desired to live. EVERY COLLEGE STUDENT IN THE WORLD NEEDS THIS BOOK!"

-Martin Elliott
Recent Graduate, Univ. of Western Ontario (London, Canada)

"Getting information and experience for a job can be baffling. No one tells you what you should do and how to do it. This book provides the kind of guidance that ALL students should be aware of."

-Mirasol Machicado
Recent Graduate, UCLA

"It doesn't surprise me that Jim would write a book like this.......a proven how to from a man who walks his talk."

-Dr. Robert L. Polk
Retired Vice President of Sales and Marketing
Allied Signal Aerospace Canada

"This book provides you with the secrets necessary to land any job! It is a MUST for anyone seeking employment."

-Jason Gigliotti
Recent Graduate, Penn State University

"I enjoyed reading this book and I recommend it highly to anyone wishing to enter the Real World of the work force. This is information many people can use!"

-Milt Jackson
Assistant Head Coach, Atlanta Falcons

"James Malinchak makes finding a job a challenge, not a chore. This book is sure to be a hit with college students."

-Garrin Hirschhorn
Recent Graduate, University of Florida

"Jim has found a way to bust the link in the catch 22 of finding that first job."

-Charley Steiner
ESPN SportsCenter

"As a former Resident Manager I received hundreds of resumes from potential applicants. Less than 1% ever followed up with a letter or a phone call. James Malinchak followed up with a barrage of letters, phone calls, and personal visits to literally nail down the position he desired. Look up perseverance in the dictionary and you'll find the definition James Malinchak. Follow his recommendations in this book and you'll be ahead of anyone else seeking the position that you desire."

-Ron Visconti
Vice President, Merrill Lynch

"This is a great book about bridging the gap between the fantasy world of college and the Real World of business. I recommend this book to anyone who really wants success!"

-John E. Kilfoyle
Senior Vice President-Investments
Dean Witter Reynolds Inc.

"In the game of football, business or life, the difference between success or failure is simply the attitude one takes. You want the intent of this attitude to be positive. Jim Malinchaks' positive attitude jumps off the pages with every word."

-Rusty Tillman
Defensive Coordinator, Tampa Bay Buccaneers

"As a General Manager I have never come across an applicant who has used these unique techniques. Follow this book and you will separate yourself from the crowd."

-Davy J. Tyburski
General Manager, Kinetic Concepts Inc. (KCI)

"Congratulations Jim, this is the greatest self help book for college students I have ever read. EVERY STUDENT MUST READ THIS BOOK!"

-Dr. Leroy Perry
5 Time Olympic Chiropractor &
President of International Sports Medicine Institute (Los Angeles)

FROM
COLLEGE
TO THE
REAL WORLD

.....How to Land ANY Job You Desire
-Right Out of College!

*"Street smart ideas and techniques
that will get you hired!"*

James Malinchak

Published by
Positive Publishing
Coral Springs, FL

Printed in the United States of America

Library of Congress Catalog Card Number: 95-71837

ISBN 0-9646924-0-6

Text editing by Gay Simmons and Suzanne Ashe
Cover graphics by Lin Alvarez

Warning - Disclaimer
The purpose of this book is to educate and entertain. This book does not promise or guarantee that anyone following the ideas, tips, suggestions, techniques or strategies will be hired. It is the discretion of employers if you will or will not be hired. The author, publisher and distributor(s) shall have neither liability nor responsibility to anyone with respect to any loss or damage caused, or alleged to be caused, directly or indirectly by the information contained in this book.

Acknowledgments

There are many people who have helped me in my life. Without their guidance, advice, and support I would not be where I am today.

To William Malinchak for always believing in me and making me believe in myself. You're a great mentor.

To my parents (Walter & Betty) for always allowing me to make my own decisions and supporting whichever path I chose to follow. I love you both dearly.

To my sister Cindy & brother Wally for growing closer after the death of Vicki and realizing how important we are to each other.

To Melanie DuBois for your love and support in the pursuit of my dreams. You're a special person.

To Davy Tyburski for your willingness to help in any manner.

To Dr. Robert L. Polk for encouraging me to strive for the top.

To Dr. William E. Wilson for all of your help throughout college and in the pursuit of my career.

To Sam Wallis for giving me my start in the financial industry.

To John Kai for continuously motivating me to succeed.

To Jase Simmons for your friendship and for believing in this book.

To Lin Alvarez for your extra effort, Gay Simmons & Suzanne Ashe-Dudley for your editing, and Carma at 5000 Plus Printing for all of your help.

To everyone who has contributed to my success. Without you, my achievements would not be possible. Thank you from the bottom of my heart.

Most of all I would like to thank GOD for giving me the inner strength to conquer life's obstacles.

This book is dedicated to my sister Vicki, who taught me to never give up when facing any obstacle.....I miss you very much
1952-1991

Contents

A Message to YOU!   11

About the Author   13

CH 1:
Are You Ready For The Real World?   15

CH 2:
How I Did It & How You Can Do It!   25

CH 3:
How To Acquire Work Experience
When You're A Full-Time Student   33

CH 4:
Writing A Resume That Will
Have Employers Calling You   46

CH 5:
Writing A Cover Letter
That Sells You & Your Resume   61

CH 6:
How To Interview Like A Pro   70

CH 7:
Following Up In A Professional
And Unique Manner   83

CH 8:
How To Separate Yourself From The Crowd   93

CH 9:
Persistence Is The Key That Will
Unlock Many Doors   98

CH 10:
Tips From Employers About Getting Hired   102

A Special Announcement   123

James is Available for Speaking Engagements   126

Rave Reviews from Colleges and Top Speakers   127

Other Books Written by James   128

A MESSAGE TO YOU!

I KNOW WHY YOU PICKED UP THIS BOOK! I was in your shoes not too long ago. You are faced with the same difficult situation that faced me and faces many other soon-to-be graduates. You are about to graduate from college and aspire to land a certain career. But you allow your age and lack of experience to convince you that it's not possible. You wonder if you should settle for any job rather than pursuing the career you truly desire.

I know what you are going through because I have been there. I understand how easy it is to give up because you think no employer will give you a chance. No one believes in you. People laugh and tell you that you are too young. And you begin to believe them. You are not alone because this has also happened to me.

YOU HAVE TWO CHOICES: (1) Believe all of those negatives and give up on pursuing the job you desire, or (2) BELIEVE IN YOURSELF and that YOU CAN LAND IT! Those are the only choices you have. If you decide to give up, please put down this book. There's no need for you to read any further. But if you truly have the desire and believe in yourself, then *YOU MUST READ ON......*

The following pages contain the most valuable information you will ever learn about getting hired. It's not taught in any college or in any other book. These techniques were developed by trial and error in the pursuit of my career.

I'm not a professor, lecturer, or researcher. I don't have a masters or doctorate degree. I'M JUST LIKE YOU! I'm an average, everyday college graduate who simply pursued and landed the job I desired despite my age, lack of experience and qualifications or advanced degrees. The strategies, techniques, and tips are offered from experience. I've gone through everything you're about to go through. As a young graduate I battled against older, more experienced and more qualified candidates. I faced and overcame the objections and rejections from employers.

The purpose of this book is to make your pursuit easier. If I can provide you with only one tip or suggestion that will help you land the job you desire then I've accomplished my goal.

This book explains exactly what to expect when competing in the (job market) "Real World." It will not waste your time with the traditional methods usually taught for pursuing a job. The strategies and techniques in this book have one objective: TO GET YOU HIRED! This is your guide that will teach you exactly how to land any job you desire right out of college.

The Real World is so different from college. I wrote this book so you'll know exactly what to expect and exactly what you must do to get hired. Too many graduates settle for any job rather than pursuing the career they truly desire. Don't be one of them.

I'm sure many of you are smarter, more educated, and better qualified than me. But if you're not ready for the Real World, it doesn't matter how smart, educated, or qualified you are. This book will not only prepare you for your battle, it will teach you how to beat out ANY candidate for ANY position.

The problem with most books written for students is that they are too long and drawn out. The last thing any student wants to do after going through a rigorous semester is to read another thick book. Remember, I was in your shoes not too long ago. I understand your thinking.

You want a guide that's simple, short and to the point, while providing powerful techniques that work! Now you have it. This book teaches exactly what you must do to separate yourself from the crowd and get hired. YOU CAN DO IT - THE TIME IS NOW!

About the Author

JAMES MALINCHAK WAS JUST LIKE YOU, an average, everyday college student who desired to land a great job right out of college. Using the techniques in his book he did it at age 23, and now he's teaching you how you can do it.

James began college at the University of Cincinnati on a basketball scholarship. He is a recent graduate of the University of Hawaii where he majored in business administration and also played college basketball. He was the only student selected to speak to his graduating class at the commencement ceremonies. Ironically, the theme of his speech was: *College is Over.....Are You Prepared for the Real World?*

Presently, at the age of 27, James is a successful stockbroker on famed Rodeo Drive in Beverly Hills, CA. He has won numerous awards including *Most Outstanding Performance* (twice) and *#1 in New Accounts* (twice). He handles the accounts of many of the world's most famous actors, entertainers, authors and professional athletes and is a frequent television and radio guest. James speaks on college campuses worldwide and is being touted as *"America's Hottest Young Speaker!"*

James is a native of Monessen, PA (near Pittsburgh) and now makes his home in the Beverly Hills area where he spends his time writing, speaking and managing investments for clients. You may contact James at:

James Malinchak International
P.O. Box 3944
Beverly Hills, CA 90212-0944
(954) 796-1925 - Email: JamesMal@aol.com
http://www.Malinchak.com

"America's Hottest Young Speaker"

Topics: (A brief overview of the points covered)

1) **From College to the Real World!**
    * Secrets to beat out any candidate for any position
    * What employers really care about and look for in candidates
    * Unique tactics to package, sell and market yourself
    * Resume writing that will make employers call you

2) **Surviving and Succeeding in College!**
    * Time management, prioritizing and forming good study habits
    * Plan your future (*FREE Success Planner* provided to students)
    * *Networking for Success* with alumni, businesses & the community
    * Commit to yourself.......not to drugs and alcohol

3) **Jump-Start Your Leadership Skills!**
    * How to effectively lead individuals and groups
    * Creating an image of a great leader
    * Developing the communication skills of a top leader
    * 3 most important rules for demonstrating great leadership

---

** Special Bonus **
Schedule James and receive 100 FREE BOOKS

James conducts over 100 presentations a year. To invite James to speak at your college or conference, contact:

(954) 796-1925 or Email: JamesMal@aol.com

14

CHAPTER 1

ARE YOU READY FOR THE REAL WORLD?

School will be finished sooner than you think and you're going to face the biggest challenge of your life, the Real World! You'll no longer be able to use the line, "I am a college student" to excuse your irresponsibilities. You'll no longer be able to rely on others for financial support. Now it's time for you to take responsibility for yourself!

First, you must realize the Real World doesn't owe you a thing. Too many graduates believe they're entitled to the job of their choice just because they've completed college. I have only two words for those of you who believe this: WAKE UP! No company will *hand* you a career just because you have a college degree.

> *"If you wake up tomorrow and believe that you can trade a college degree for the perfect job, go back to sleep - it was just a bad dream."*
>
> -UNKNOWN

Remember, you're about to graduate from college and lack extensive experience. In fact, many seasoned professionals consider you to be unqualified and immature. Therefore, it's up to you to create your own opportunities.

But how can you achieve this? How can a person fresh out of college compete in such a competitive job market against individuals with five, ten, or even twenty years of experience?

THIS BOOK WILL BE YOUR GUIDE. It's the single source of information on everything you need to know about getting yourself hired.

IDENTIFY YOUR IDEAL CAREER

Before plunging into the competitive job market, you must identify you ideal career. You need a clear idea of the precise career you truly desire. After all, how can you attain something if you don't know what that something is?

Ask yourself the following two questions. They'll help you to crystalize the career you most desire.

1)   What career really excites and energizes me?

2)   What career would make me feel the most fulfilled?

Upon answering these questions you'll have identified your ideal career; the job you truly desire.

Once you've identified your ideal career, make a commitment to yourself to pursue your ambition. And don't allow others to sabotage your desires. Many people dream of working a certain job or in a particular industry. But few accomplish their dream because they listen when others tell them it's not possible.

You have the ability within yourself to pursue and land any job you desire. Don't listen to those who try to discourage you. These are probably the very people who have never, and will never land their ideal career. Just because they haven't done it they think that you can't either. They're wrong! Although it may be a difficult task, YOU CAN DO IT!

3 KEY PRINCIPLES

Landing the position you desire right out of college will be a difficult, but not an impossible, task. Before starting the pursuit of your career you must mentally prepare yourself for the objections and setbacks that await you. You must be focused on your objectives and your plan for achieving them. And you must believe that nothing will stop you from landing your career. You can prepare yourself by understanding the following 3 KEY PRINCIPLES:

Principle #1
YOU MUST OVERCOME OBSTACLES

"History has demonstrated that the most notable winners usually encounter heartbreaking obstacles before they triumphed. They won because they refused to become discouraged by their defeats."

-B.C. FORBES

When you begin your job search you will face obstacles. Obstacles such as your age, lack of experience and lack of qualifications. Employers will not take you seriously. Friends may even laugh at you for trying to pursue a certain career. Prepare yourself because these are the very obstacles that await you. The choice is yours as to whether you'll allow these obstacles to stop you from pursuing your career.

How well you succeed in the pursuit of your job will depend, first, on your willingness to overcome these and any other obstacles that you face. You will face these minor setbacks because it happens to most students. It's a part of the job hunt. The question is who will overcome them? Those who realize that these obstacles exist and those who have the persistence to overcome them generally go on to land the position they're pursuing.

Principle #2
YOU MUST SET GOALS FOR YOURSELF

"If you don't know where you are going, how can you expect to get there?"

-BASIL S. WALSH

The purpose of goals is to focus your attention. You will not reach toward achievement until you have a clear picture of what your goals are. Identifying reachable objectives gives you the targets for achieving these goals. This will ignite a fire inside that makes you desire to achieve your objectives. Once this desire is felt, your determination to succeed becomes more powerful than any feeling to give up.

It's imperative that you set goals before your job search. Not having goals is like trying to drive a car without a road map to a state you've never visited. How can you expect to reach your destination without proper direction? The same holds true for pursuing your goal of landing a job. You need a plan; your road map. Plan your course of action step by step.

"If you fail to plan you're planning to fail."

-UNKNOWN

Principle #3
YOU MUST BELIEVE IN YOURSELF

"The mind is the limit. As long as the mind can envision the fact that you can do something, you can do it - as long as you really believe it 100%."

-UNKNOWN

Believing in yourself is the most important principle you <u>must</u> adopt before starting your job search. When you begin pursuing your job, you'll meet people who say you aren't qualified or experienced enough. You'll meet employers who think you're too young, immature and naive. You'll meet people who tell you that you don't have the ability to succeed. And you'll meet others who just don't believe in you. So if you don't believe in yourself, who will?

"A great pleasure in life is doing what people say you cannot do."

-WALTER GAGEHOT

19

There is no better feeling than when you truly believe that you will accomplish your goal(s). Your confidence level rises, obstacles disappear, and your dreams become reality.

Although there are many principles you can adopt that will help prepare you for your job search, OVERCOMING OBSTACLES, SETTING GOALS, and BELIEVING IN YOURSELF are vital. If you adopt these 3 KEY PRINCIPLES there's no reason why you can't land any position you desire.

WHEN TO BEGIN YOUR JOB SEARCH

Hopefully you're reading this book prior to your senior year. You must begin thinking, now, how to better your chances of being hired after graduation. Gaining experience in your field of study is an excellent way of accomplishing this. You can gain experience by participating in an internship. Chapter three will get into more detail about the advantages of interning.

If you're not reading this book before your senior year don't worry. The strategies and techniques will definitely help you. But I suggest you gain some type of experience in your field of study before graduation. Even if it's only for a few weeks. At least you'll have some experience to list on your resume.

Most students begin pursuing a job one or two months before graduation. If this is your plan you're making a big mistake. Think about how many students will be competing in the job market at that time. And don't forget about those who are currently working in the Real World who may be pursuing other positions. The market can become saturated with candidates around graduation.

The sooner you begin pursuing your job the more of an advantage you'll have. When mapping out your plan, take the following into consideration.

Developing a quality resume should take approximately one month. As you'll learn in chapters four and five the resume and cover letter are the initial contact with employers. It's essential to develop quality material.

You should plan on interviewing approximately six months before graduation. This may seem inappropriate, since you'll not graduate for another six months. But, it's more beneficial to get your name known to employers early. Remember, you're going to be fresh out of college. Employers will show more interest in experienced and qualified candidates. But as you'll learn in chapters seven, eight, and nine persisting for six months will make employers realize just how much you want the job. A candidate's desire for a position means a lot to employers.

YOU MUST SELL YOURSELF

"The most marketable asset you possess is YOU!"

-UNKNOWN

Before preparing for your job search you must understand the phrase *Perception Is Reality!* How people perceive you is how they tend to believe you actually are. Think of your own perception of people when you first meet them. Immediately you begin to form judgments from the clothes they wear, how they speak, their facial expressions, etc... Everyone forms these judgments, especially employers.

Since employers will form personal judgments about candidates, you must do everything possible to make a positive impression. Remember, you will compete against more experienced and more qualified candidates. The bottom line is you must *sell* yourself better than the other candidates.

It's not as difficult as it sounds. You need only an understanding of what to expect, adequate preparation, and a plan with a willingness to follow through.

21

First, determine which qualities employers may be looking for in candidates. Then, simply adopt and convey these qualities whenever you come in contact with employers.

When I began my job search, I desired to work for Merrill Lynch as a stockbroker. I knew that Merrill Lynch usually does not hire individuals who don't have at least five to ten years of business experience. I had to find a way to get noticed by employers.

I talked with various Merrill Lynch brokers to learn exactly what management looks for in potential candidates. I believed that candidates would need a substantial financial background and years of sales experience in the financial industry. But amazingly, every broker agreed that management looked for candidates who possessed the following qualities:

- the desire to succeed
- the dedication to work hard
- the willingness to overcome setbacks
- the ability to set and finish tasks
- the belief that they would achieve
- a positive mental attitude
- a likable personality
- a professional appearance
- adequate communication skills

None of these qualities required further education to gain more financial knowledge. These were qualities that could be developed by anyone and conveyed to employers.

I lacked the five to ten years of business experience usually required by Merrill Lynch. But I did develop all of the above positive qualities and I worked hard to sell employers on these qualities so they would perceive that I was a superior candidate.

You're probably wondering if employers in other industries look for the same, or similar qualities? Of course they do. If Merrill Lynch, one of the most stable and well respected firms in the world, looks for these qualities in candidates don't you think other firms do also?

Most employers don't search for candidates who have an in-depth knowledge of a particular industry. Hired candidates will be trained and will gain that knowledge. Employers can't teach the personal qualities mentioned above. When they meet a candidate who possesses these qualities they're usually motivated to find a position for that individual.

Conveying these qualities to employers is exactly what you must do to sell yourself. Any employer can be sold on a candidate who conveys them. Selling employers on YOU must be your main objective. You will not win them over with your experience or qualifications because, in reality, yours are not as impressive as experienced candidates. But YOU CAN convey the above positive qualities to employers, thus, making them regard you in a very positive manner.

"YOU CAN DO IT!"

CHAPTER 2

HOW I DID IT &
HOW YOU CAN DO IT!

I've always wanted to work in the financial industry. Helping people to manage and invest their money has always been my ideal career. I would often find myself daydreaming about being a young hot-shot, *wheeling-n-dealing* in the business world. Even today, I still daydream some of those exact thoughts.

It's good to daydream every now and then. Dreaming allows us to visualize what we desire most. It allows us to form a mental picture of how fulfilled we would be upon realizing our vision. The problem with dreaming is that most people tend to think their dream can never be real.

I was one of those people until my junior year in high school. A high school teacher, whom I respected highly, once made a comment that truly changed my attitude. Mrs. Monaghan said, "You can do anything that you put your mind to. IF YOU CAN DREAM IT, YOU CAN DO IT!"

From that moment on I've never settled for anything less than my dreams. If I envisioned achieving something then I pursued it until it was achieved. I'm the same way today and will always be that way. Anything that I've ever accomplished in my life began with me, first, dreaming about it.

Dreaming and believing that you will realize your dream is half the battle. Once you become determined to achieve your dream nothing will stop you.

> *"Some men dream of worthy accomplishments, while others stay awake and do them."*
>
> -UNKNOWN

HOW IT ALL BEGAN

I grew up in Monessen, PA a small steel-mill town located near Pittsburgh. The economic environment in that area is not what you would call positive. Jobs are scarce while employment continues to decline. Even the largest employer and revenue producing company, Wheeling Pittsburgh Steel, has downsized its employment.

Growing up in a city like Monessen seems to bring out the best in some people. Our small town has produced actors and actresses, professional football players, corporate executives, and even a World Heavyweight Boxing Champion. It may seem amazing that people of this magnitude would come from such a small town. However, growing up in a place with a declining economy seems to motivate certain people to achieve their dreams. At least that's how it began for me.

OFF TO COLLEGE

My first big dream was to play college basketball for a major university. I often envisioned playing on television and in sold out arenas. But as others became aware of my goal, many laughed and said it couldn't be done. I heard all of the reasons why I would fail.....not quick enough, not fast enough, doesn't shoot well enough, doesn't have the athletic ability, plays at a small high school, comes from a small town, no one else has ever done it so how could he? But what those people didn't realize was that I had a dream and nothing would stop me from realizing it.

My dream was fulfilled when I accepted a basketball scholarship to the University of Cincinnati. My vision of playing on television and in sold out arenas became a reality. Those who once told me that it couldn't be done were now envious because I didn't fall into their trap of negativity. I didn't listen to their reasons why I should fail. I simply believed in myself and focused my mind on the pursuit of my dream. I didn't care if no one believed in me. All that mattered was that I believed in myself and that I wouldn't quit until I realized my dream.

I spent a short time at Cincinnati before transferring to the University of Hawaii to complete my academic and athletic career. Attending college in Hawaii would seem to be a dream-come-true for anyone.

27

It certainly was for me. I found myself more relaxed and appreciating the simple things that life had to offer.....warm weather, beautiful flowers, the sound of the ocean.

GAINING EXPERIENCE DURING COLLEGE

Ever since the tenth grade I've always dreamed of becoming a stockbroker. The business has always fascinated me and the thought of helping people to achieve their financial goals energized me. I've always felt that helping people to manage and invest their money is such an important profession, just as is medicine or the law.

The summer before my junior year of college a relative, William Malinchak, suggested that I do an internship in the financial industry. I began thinking about life after college and realized this would be a great opportunity to gain experience. And just the thought of being involved in this industry made my heart accelerate.

I decided to search for a job that would look impressive on my resume. So I pursued and landed a position on the New York Commodity Exchange (COMEX) in New York City. I sacrificed my entire summer vacation so that, in the future, I could list the experience on my resume.

My position on the COMEX was a *runner*, which meant doing whatever my boss needed done - whether it was working on commodity trades or getting him a cup of coffee. I was more concerned about learning from trained professionals than about earning money. The education I received from this experience was worth much more than any money earned. In addition, I had an impressive job to list on my resume and an employer willing to provide a quality recommendation on my behalf.

After such a positive experience on the COMEX, I decided to search for another internship for the summer before my senior year. I was finishing my education at the University of Hawaii and needed to remain at school to take a few summer courses in order to graduate the following May.

After browsing through the telephone book I mailed my resume, along with a cover letter, to all of the brokerage firms in the area. I only received one positive reply, which was from Mr. Sam Wallis, Vice President and Office Manager of Merrill Lynch in Hilo, HI.

A few days later we met for an interview. At the end of the interview Mr. Wallis said that Merrill Lynch usually does not offer internships to college students. However, he was so impressed with the interview that he hired me as his personal assistant and paid me out of his own pocket. I now had two jobs relative to my field of interest to build my resume and two employers willing to provide recommendations.

Interning at Merrill Lynch turned out to be the most important career decision I've ever made. Mr. Wallis opened the door for my employment with Merrill Lynch after graduation. He knew the office manager in the office where I desired to work and called to offer a recommendation on my behalf. Mr. Wallis told him that he would hire me if I desired to live in Hawaii after graduation. The office manager became interested in hiring me. And eventually he did!

MY INSPIRATION

It is said that everyone has an inspiration in their life. It may be a motivational talk from someone you respect. Or an experience that you have. Whatever the inspiration it teaches you to look at life from a different perspective.

My inspiration occurred a month before I was to depart for college in Hawaii. My sister, Vicki, collapsed one evening with the right side of her body paralyzed. The initial indication was that she had suffered a stroke. But test results confirmed it was much more serious. There was a malignant brain tumor causing her paralysis. Her doctors didn't give her more than three months to live. I remember wondering how this could happen? A few weeks before she collapsed Vicki was perfectly fine. And now her life was coming to an end at such a young age.

29

The day before my scheduled departure I had mixed emotions about leaving. Part of me said to forget about college and stay there with Vicki. The other part said to finish my education. I was unsure about what to do.

It was getting late and I had to make a decision. Only Vicki and I were in her hospital room. I made the mistake of telling her that I might not leave for college. She became angry and told me I had better finish my education. Vicki said she would be fine and not to worry about her. There was Vicki lying ill in a hospital bed telling me not to worry.

Leaving that evening, knowing it was the last time I'd see her alive, was the most difficult thing I've ever done. Before leaving, Vicki made me promise never to give up fighting against any obstacle in my life. Again, there she was lying ill in a hospital bed encouraging me. It didn't seem fair that such a wonderful person had to go through this agony.

Vicki passed away on November 29, 1991 living a month longer than her doctors had expected her to live. The doctors couldn't give an explanation how she overcame the odds and lived this long. They didn't have to because I already knew the answer. She did it because she never gave up fighting to overcome her obstacle........

Vicki inspired me to never give up even when the odds seem impossible. If you believe you will win then you will. Vicki proved that by living longer than she was expected to live. She won! And because of her I know I'll win against any obstacle I face. I learned always to pursue my dreams, never giving up until they're realized. Life is too short to settle for anything less. And your dreams are not difficult to realize if you NEVER GIVE UP the pursuit!

LANDING THE CAREER I DESIRED

The beginning of my senior year was when I began to think seriously about life after college. The arrival of the senior year has a motivating effect. You begin to panic as you realize the Real World is fast approaching.

My ambition was to work in the financial industry for a major corporation. However, the odds were certainly against me landing such a significant position right out of college. I had little experience, few qualifications and was only 23 years old. Who would even think of hiring someone with my credentials?

But I had a dream. And as I said before, I'll never allow myself to settle for anything less than my dreams. I decided that I was going to get hired by one of the largest investing firms in the industry. I didn't care how many objections or roadblocks I'd meet along the way, I would not stop until I realized my dream. I developed a plan with a strategy to follow and I mentally prepared myself for the rigorous competition I was about to face. I'm not going to tell you that my road was an easy drive. But, by using the strategies and techniques in this book, I DID IT!

IF I DID IT, YOU CAN DO IT

For those of you trying to decide between settling for any job you can find or pursuing the job you truly desire, I have one last thing to say. You and I are no different. No one handed me my career on a silver platter. There was no magic formula, no rich relative, no miracle. Just a desire and determination to achieve a dream. Anyone can do that. It doesn't take the most educated or the most experienced person. It only takes a person willing to overcome obstacles, set goals, and believe in themselves. I'm not going to tell you that your pursuit will be easy. But if you're willing to persist without giving up while never losing focus of your vision, then you WILL land any career you desire.

If I did it, YOU CAN DO IT!

"BELIEVE IN YOURSELF!"

CHAPTER 3

HOW TO ACQUIRE WORK EXPERIENCE WHEN YOU'RE A FULL-TIME STUDENT

Today most employers want to hire candidates who possess quality experience. Hiring experienced candidates allows for less training costs and a lower turnover rate (people leaving the company).

As you begin thinking about pursuing a career, realize that you will compete against experienced individuals. If you were an employer, who would you hire? The recent college graduate with no experience or the experienced professional? Prepare yourself because you will face this challenge.

Now that I've worried you with the fact that you will face stiff competition, let me also give you a positive note. You can compete and prevail if you're willing to gain hands on experience.

You're probably wondering how a full-time college student can possibly gain quality experience? The answer is by performing an internship in your field of interest. This experience will show employers that you've learned basic knowledge of the field while allowing you to interact with Real World professionals. In addition, it will convey the fact that you're serious about pursuing a career in that industry. Employers love to hire young, serious, hard working individuals. Interning is a great way to convey that you're this type of individual.

INTERNING IS THE KEY

Most colleges and universities offer internship programs that allow students to work in their chosen field of study while receiving academic credit for doing so. You can earn approximately 12-15 credits for participating in such programs.

Fortunately, most colleges offer financial assistance and encourage students to participate. The college receives exposure from having their students interacting in the professional world.

If your college doesn't offer internship programs, take the initiative and telephone employers to inquire about the possibility of interning.

If they don't hire college students for employment, volunteer to work for free a few hours a week. I can't imagine any employer declining an individual offering to work for free.

Your objective is to gain experience. Don't allow whether or not you'll be paid to determine if you intern. The experience will be worth much more than the income. You'll gain experience, build your resume, and establish quality contacts. These three factors will be extremely important when pursuing a job after graduation.

Grades are no longer as important in the hiring process. Although maintaining a quality grade point average is an indication of success, employers are more concerned about your experience. Victor Lindquist, Northwestern's dean of placement, once commented, "Because training programs have been cut back, internships are more important than ever" (*Money* magazine, June 1994).

Most internships are performed during a semester of college. However, you should also consider interning during the summer months. The summer is no time to fool around. My junior high school basketball coach once made a comment that has always stuck out in my mind. Coach Marino said, "Good basketball players develop their skills in the summer, not during the season, so work hard to improve this summer."

The same philosophy applies to gaining work experience. Don't waste your summers. Many employers look for summer help. But with the end of the semester arriving, you may not hear of the potential positions available. Take the initiative and contact employers about interning the summer for them.

Make sure to work a job that relates to your field of study. Many students work summer jobs and earn decent money. But certain jobs may not help them to land a position in their field of interest. For example, a job as a lifeguard may be enjoyable but will not help you to land a computer position after graduation.

The importance of internships can't be stressed enough. You're making a big mistake if you choose not to pursue them. Students nationwide have testified to the benefits and opportunities gained from interning. Rather than rambling on about the importance of internships I thought I'd conclude this section by listing real-life examples. I interviewed various students from across the country, asking for their comments. Amazingly, every student agreed that the experience and benefits gained from interning is the key to securing a job after graduation.

YVETTE GALLARDO, a communications major at the **University of Southern California (USC),** interned for both NBC Studios and Tri-Star Pictures to learn more about the entertainment industry and to meet quality contacts. She worked in the media relations department and frequently covered such shows as *The Tonight Show* and *Days of Our Lives*. Yvette commented, "I was involved with many different aspects of marketing and promotions of film and I really learned a lot."

When asked what she would recommend to students thinking of pursuing internships Yvette replied, "Internships are the only way to get experience and meet people while you're in college. Get as much experience as possible and go for a big name place that you're really excited about. You have to be excited about going to work everyday."

GARRIN HIRSCHHORN, a sociology major at the **University of Florida,** interned for Atlantic Records in Gainesville, FL to try to break into the recording industry. He described his internship as an overall positive experience. "I did my internship to get my foot in the door in the record business. It's such a difficult industry to get into unless you know someone of influence. Even though I worked for free I've made many good contacts and I've gained Real World experience."

When asked what he would recommend to students thinking about pursuing internships Garrin replied, "The most important thing to do when pursuing something is to be persistent, don't take no for an answer. Experiment with any possible avenue to get the internship you really want."

MANUEL SIGALA, a management information systems major at the **University of Texas,** interned at Bank of America. Manuel commented on how the internship was an overall positive experience. "I was exposed to the working environment and how the Real World operates. I learned skills that will be valuable later in my career. The really good thing about internships is that you meet influential people who will always want to help you in the future."

When asked what he would recommend to students considering internships Manuel replied, "Start early because it will help you determine which field you really want to pursue. It may be different in the Real World from what you learn in the classroom about a particular career. Also, you have to get the most out of your internship so treat it as if it were your full-time job."

JEFF HACKETT, a communications and sales marketing major at **California State University-Northridge,** worked in the marketing industry for the overall benefits gained from internships. "I wanted a position where I could build skills and get experience. The internship taught me how to deal with customers and clients while helping to build my communication skills. Because of how I developed, I began getting job offers. Employers were telling me to contact them when I finished school. I made sure to keep their business cards."

Jeff offers the following advice to students thinking of pursuing internships. "It's useless while you're in college to work a useless job. Don't work just to earn money. Work to learn skills that will help you when you graduate. Having a degree isn't that big of a deal. Thousands of people have degrees. What counts is having a degree and experience."

GREG HART, an economics major at the **University of Pittsburgh,** interned for Shearson Lehman Brothers to learn more about the stock brokerage industry. The experience proved to be more beneficial than he first anticipated. "When I interviewed for jobs after graduation, I was asked more about my internship than my grades. Employers wanted to know what I did and what I learned. They were very interested in the internship."

Greg's chances of securing a position with Shearson Lehman Brothers after graduation increased tremendously because of his internship. Greg said, "After my junior year of college, Shearson was already offering me a position over more experienced people."

When asked what he would recommend to students thinking of pursuing internships Greg replied, "Start early. The more experience you can gain through interning the better chance you have of getting hired by that company after graduation."

WAYNE RIEGER, a history major at the *University of Cincinnati,* decided during college that he wanted to pursue a career in athletics. He worked for the university athletic department and learned what it takes to arrange athletic events. "I conducted various jobs which gave me experience in the operations side of athletic events. It put me in daily contact with other personnel in the athletic department and I was able to see how the different offices operated."

In addition to gaining quality experience, Wayne was able to establish contacts that proved to be an important factor when he pursued a position with the university athletic department after graduation. "I got to know the athletic department people well and I would frequently talk to those who worked in the areas that I had an interest. They knew me and felt comfortable with hiring me."

Wayne offers the following advice to those thinking about pursuing an internship, "You have to intern, it's ideal. Work experience is definitely more of a factor in the pursuit of your job than grades. No one ever asked me about my grades when I interviewed."

TINA TENRET, an international affairs major at the *University of Virginia,* interned on the *Today Show* at NBC Studios. The contacts she has developed will certainly be helpful in the pursuit of her dream job as a television news anchor. Tina remarked, "I talked with Katie Couric and Bryant Gumble who are the co-anchors of the Today Show. Also, I've met and worked with several producers and even the Executive Producer who runs the Today Show."

Tina has also gained quality experience about the television industry and definitely recommends internships to all students. "I got to see all aspects of how a specific show is produced. I've learned everything from dubbing tapes to what it takes to actually air the show. Internships are absolutely the best way to get a head start on a career before you pursue an actual job."

AMEENA MAJID, a political science and journalism major at the *University of Iowa,* interned for Pinkerton Risk Assessment Services in Washington, DC to learn more about international relations. Ameena believes that interning was a very positive experience. "Interning provided me with personal growth and experience in international relations. It taught me how to communicate with people in the work place and prepared me for what to expect when I get out of college."

When asked what she would recommend to students thinking of pursuing internships Ameena replied, "Before pursuing an internship you need to do a good self-assessment of your abilities and what it is you want out of your internship. This will be the step right before your career so you must do a good self-assessment of what you want to do and where you want to be after graduation. Don't just pick an internship because someone recommended it. Make sure you will be able to get everything out of your internship that you want to."

TONY BROYLES, a logistics and transportation major at the *University of Tennessee,* interned for Dana Corporation in Knoxville, TN. When asked to comment on how his internship was beneficial Tony replied, "It helped me a lot. I was able to see the business side of my major rather than just what I learned in the classroom. I gained good experience that others didn't. It helped me a lot in getting my current position."

When asked if he would recommend internships to other students Tony replied, "Absolutely! I have in the past and I do to everyone that I talk to. I tell them to start early and not to be afraid to call employers on their own to see what they offer. Also, I tell them not to be afraid of going away to another city or state to perform an internship."

MIKE CHVALA, a mechanical engineering major at **Gannon University** (Erie, PA), interned with ARMCO Advanced Materials in Butler, PA to gain Real World experience in the industrial design field. Mike said that interning allowed him to interact with quality contacts. "I worked for the Senior Engineer who hired me to handle some of his less difficult projects. I'm sure I'll get a good recommendation from him and the other engineers in the company. I've also gotten to know people from other companies."

When asked if he would recommend internships to other students Mike replied, "Definitely! The experience is excellent and employers look for that when you interview."

BETH RIPPLE, a communications management major at the **University of Portland,** interned for OMSI (Oregon Museum of Science and Industry) to learn more about the special events industry. Beth said that interning allowed her to network with people in the industry. "I made several contacts in the industry throughout the area. In addition, I have great references from the people I worked for at OMSI. I even went on a few interviews and because OMSI is well known in the Portland area, employers became very interested in me."

When asked what she would recommend to students thinking of pursuing internships Beth replied, "You should definitely do internships, especially non-paying ones. They show that you're very serious and would do anything to get into that industry."

CHRISTINE ENCINAS, an engineering student at **Jacksonville University** (Jacksonville, FL) interned for the United Parcel Service to learn more about the industrial engineering field. Christine described her overall positive experience. "I've gained much more hands-on computer experience than I could ever learn in the classroom and I always have managers and supervisors asking me what my future plans are. I'm positive they will try to do as much as possible to help me after graduation."

When asked if she would recommend internships to other students Christine replied, "I definitely would recommend them! You gain a lot of experience and you mature faster. You definitely see what happens out there in the Real World. Be sure to get the most out of your internship. The experience will be very beneficial."

MIRASOL MACHICADO, a psychology major at *UCLA,* interned at Verdugo Woodland Elementary School in Glendale, CA to learn more about the field she desires to work in. Mirasol offered the following comments on her experience. "I thought it would give me the experience I would need for the Real World. I felt I needed to be submerged in the field that I wanted to get into. I was able to see things that I wouldn't have been able to see in an educational setting (classroom). It opened my eyes to a lot of things I wasn't aware of and it allowed me to see if the field was really what I wanted to get into."

When asked if she would recommend internships to other students Mirasol replied, "Definitely! It opens your eyes to what it's really like to work in the field you've chosen. What my internship did for me was to narrow down what the exact title (position) is that I wanted. Do your research to find out what you really want."

STEPHEN WILSON, a management information systems major at the *University of Texas,* interned as a computer programmer for the Internal Revenue Service (IRS). Stephen offered his comments about the internship. "I gained experience in my field of computers and it gave me a good feel of what the programming field is all about. The internship is something that will definitely build my resume."

When asked what he would recommend to students considering internships Stephen replied, "Perform an internship you'll enjoy.

41

Look at the overall benefits to you. You have to consider the experience you'll gain and who you might meet. Look for the internship that will help you the most, one that will help you in the long-run."

DAVID MILAVEC, an accounting major at **Duquesne University** (Pittsburgh, PA), interned for Exler Company in Pittsburgh to gain experience in the accounting field. David offered his comments about the internship. "It was definitely a positive experience because I gained experience that I wouldn't have gotten elsewhere. I gained experience in taxes and just basic accounting. Also, I went on to work there. They offered me a job a couple of months after I graduated."

David felt that interning for Exler provided him with a big advantage when he pursued a position after graduation. David commented, "They got a chance to know me. And when the time came that they needed to hire someone I was right there. They liked my work and the way I interacted with the other people so I was hired."

When asked what he would recommend to students thinking about pursuing internships David replied, "I'd definitely say to start early and beef up on your communication skills, resume writing skills, and basic writing skills because those are very important also."

As you can see from the real-life experiences listed, students nationwide recommend internships. It doesn't matter what your major is, which college you attend, where you live, or what year of school you're in - the key is to get Real World experience. You'll build your resume, gain experience, and meet quality contacts. If you choose not to intern, you're making a big mistake!

NETWORKING IS THE KEY TO YOUR FUTURE

Interning will put you in situations to meet successful people. Take advantage of the opportunity. Get to know as many people as possible. You never know who is influential or who knows who. I'm a firm believer that in today's society, who you know can help get you ahead faster than anything else. It's an unfortunate situation, but it is a reality.

Talk with successful people, even take them to lunch. Tell them you're interested in learning more about their company, their industry, how they got started in their business, or my favorite, how they became successful. People love to talk about themselves and will most likely welcome the chance to talk with you.

More important than meeting people is staying in contact. Meeting a person once will not help you in the future. You need to build a relationship by becoming friends. Get their address and phone number and stay in touch.

Send thank you notes, birthday cards, Christmas cards, Thanksgiving cards, anniversary cards, and basic letters. Call them periodically and if you happen to be in their area take them to lunch or at least stop by for a quick visit.

You need to network, not only for job purposes, but for outside interests also. Take the initiative to introduce yourself to people, become friends then, most importantly, stay in touch. You never know where it may lead.

Here's an example. I had a childhood friend named Michael. We would hang out as kids playing basketball and football. As we entered high school, my goals led me toward pursuing a college basketball scholarship while Michael's led him toward pursuing a boxing career.

After high school graduation, our paths headed in two separate directions. Michael moved to Detroit to train for boxing while I played college basketball at the University of Cincinnati and later at the University of Hawaii.

After graduating college and moving to Los Angeles to begin my brokerage career, I happened to read the following headline in a local newspaper: *Evander Holyfield to defend World Heavyweight Boxing Title against Michael Moorer.* I couldn't believe it. My childhood friend was about to fight for the heavyweight title.

I called a mutual friend of ours back in our hometown to find out if he knew how to get in touch with Michael. He did. Michael was staying at Caesars Palace Resort & Casino in Las Vegas.

I was able to get a message to Michael, leaving my phone number. I thought he probably would not remember our childhood friendship. But he did and returned my call. He said it was nice to hear from an old friend and was shocked by my call.

I promised Michael that I would be there for his big day. He told me to call him when I arrived so I could visit with him before the fight. Which I did.

Michael defeated Evander Holyfield to become the World Heavyweight Boxing Champion and I was there to witness it. All because of a simple contact and friendship made twelve years ago.

Introduce yourself to people, get their address and phone number, then stay in touch! Trust me it works. If you're skeptical, here's proof.

About a year and a half ago I was in the buffet line at a dinner party, and I noticed that Dennis Hopper, famous actor in *Speed, Waterworld* and the NIKE shoe commercials for the NFL, was also in line. He left the buffet line and sat at a table that had an open seat right next to him. This was my big chance to really test my networking skills.

After taking a deep breath I walked over to Dennis and asked him if the seat next to him was taken. It wasn't so I sat down and began eating. I was a little nervous about introducing myself. After all why would a successful person like Dennis Hopper want to talk with a young 24 year old "kid?"

But this was my big chance and I wasn't about to blow it. I took another deep breath and introduced myself while extending my hand to shake his. To my surprise, Dennis smiled, shook my hand and initiated a conversation. For the next hour, we talked about everything form sports to travel to movies.

As Dennis was leaving, I asked him for his address and phone number. To my surprise, he was happy to give it to me. He is truly a wonderful, genuine, and down-to-earth person.

Since that time, I have stayed in touch with Dennis. He even invited me to visit the set of *Waterworld* in Hawaii to watch part of the filming. Which I did. Dennis gave me a personal tour of parts of the set and even invited me to have lunch in his trailer.

Now do you believe that introducing yourself to people, getting their address and phone number, and staying in touch works?

I've been fortunate to meet some pretty well-known individuals, simply by introducing myself to people and staying in contact.

Here are a few examples: First Lady Hillary Clinton, Speaker of the House Newt Gingrich, talk show hosts Larry King and Arsenio Hall, author Mary Higgins Clark, various professional basketball (NBA), football (NFL) & baseball (MLB) players, comedian "Super Dave" Osbourne, Dr. Ruth, and actors Kiefer Sutherland and Sean Penn.

Introduce yourself to people and stay in touch with everyone that you meet. This includes childhood friends, high school friends, college friends, teachers, professors, business associates, your parents friends, your relative's friends, people you intern with, people you intern for - EVERYONE!

You Just Never Know Where It Could Lead..........

CHAPTER 4

WRITING A RESUME THAT WILL HAVE EMPLOYERS CALLING YOU

There's no official way to write a resume. If you asked the opinion of ten people you'll probably get ten different opinions. The resume must advertise, market, and sell you. It must grab the attention and interest the employer in learning more about you.

The resume has one objective: to get you an interview. Let's face it, a resume listing college activities may not be impressive to employers who have associated with experienced individuals for years. Remember two things when drafting your resume:

1) You will not receive a job offer based on your resume alone.

2) You're a student. Your resume cannot compete against those listing extensive experience and qualifications.

To get an interview you <u>must</u> draft a creative tool that will interest employers and make them *perceive* you to be an exceptional candidate. The following are suggestions for creating a resume that *sells*.

RESUME SUGGESTIONS

1) <u>LIMIT IT TO ONE PAGE</u>: Employers review many resumes and will not read a long, drawn out resume consisting of many pages. Only list the major points. An old cliche' states, *"Sometimes Less Is More."*

2) <u>MAKE IT DETAILED</u>: Resumes are skimmed, not read. Studies indicate that employers generally only skim a resume for approximately 20 seconds. Outline your resume in a simple format so employers can easily locate the important facts.

3) <u>TYPEFACE</u>: Always use the same typeface and size. Use 12 Point Times New Roman (the same format this book is typed in) because of its professional look. Don't use different sizes. It will not look professional.

4) <u>INK & PAPER COLOR</u>: Your resume should be printed in black ink and on a conservative colored paper (white, off white, ivory, grey, etc...). Make sure the paper is good quality.

5) <u>HIGHLIGHT CERTAIN AREAS</u>: Highlight the areas that you want to stand out by CAPITALIZING, *ITALICIZING,* and using **BOLD-FACE** type. The employers eyes will be drawn to these areas. Underlining doesn't look as professional and isn't recommended.

6) <u>ALIGN ALL COLUMNS</u>: Your resume will be difficult to read if not properly aligned. In addition, it may look "sloppy." Remember, you're trying to make a positive and professional impression.

7) <u>CHECK YOUR SPELLING</u>: Nothing is worse than misspelling words on your resume. There's absolutely no excuse for doing so. A misspelling shows carelessness and will create a negative image with the employer. Your resume could get tossed in the trash if there's a misspelling.

CREATING YOUR RESUME

When creating your resume always remember one important point: Employers only care about what you can do for the firm. How will you benefit the company? They're not concerned about what can be done for you.

WHAT YOUR RESUME SHOULD CONTAIN

- Heading
- Objective
- Qualifications
- Professional Experience
- Qualifications Gained
(from your professional experience)
- Education

HEADING

The heading should contain your name, address and telephone number.

NAME

Your name should be **CAPITALIZED** using **BOLD-FACE** type. Don't type it larger than other words. It may cause the employer to think you have an ego problem. Be proud of yourself but don't encourage the employer to throw your resume away because of the impression that you have an ego problem. You want your name to stand out, yet be elegantly simple.

(Example) The Mona Lisa is a great work of art that's acknowledged by the entire world. Yet it isn't flamboyant with bright splashes of color. Its elegance is in its subtlety.

ADDRESS & TELEPHONE NUMBER

Some believe you should list both your school and permanent address. I recommend using only the permanent address for two reasons:

1)   You want your resume limited to one page and detailed for easy reading (skimming), so omit any unnecessary wording. One address is sufficient.

2)   Remember, the main objective of your resume is to get you an interview. You don't want to remind employers that you're a student by listing your school address.

(FORMAT)

Type your heading in a stationary format. This will allow your resume to be unique from the traditional formats and will portray a more businesslike-professional image. The following is an example:

ROBERT A. STEWART
4 Malia Street / Hilo, HI 96720 / (808) 555-1212

OBJECTIVE

An objective tells employers the position you're pursuing. The objective should be the actual job you're pursuing or a closely related position, and should be the first item listed under the heading.

The objective is a good place to perk the employers interest. You want them to begin thinking, "This is someone I may be interested in."

Begin with your specific objective and conclude with successful words that sell your positive qualities. The following are a few examples:

OBJECTIVE: An entry level brokerage position with a retail investment firm that values superior sales ability, quality quantitative skills, and outstanding experience.

The specific objective was:	"An entry level brokerage position with a retail investment firm"
The successful words were:	"superior, quality, outstanding"
The positive qualities were:	"sales ability, quantitative skills, experience"

OBJECTIVE: An entry level management position with a nationwide firm that values outstanding leadership, quality organizational skills, and extensive experience.

The specific objective was:	"An entry level management position with a nationwide firm"
The successful words were:	"outstanding, quality, extensive"
The positive qualities were:	"leadership, organizational skills, experience"

QUALIFICATIONS

The qualifications section should coincide with the objective. List what you've learned from your past work experience that qualifies you for the position you're pursuing. Remember, employers want to know what you can do for the firm. List the qualities being looked for while describing them with proactive words. This section should be short and direct. You want to draw employers into your resume.

Using proactive words will show you're a person of action, someone who can get the job done. Use such words as:

- acquired	- handled
- administered	- honed
- analyzed	- learned
- demonstrated	- maintained
- developed	- managed
- displayed	- organized
- earned	- progressed
- excelled	- reviewed
- formed	- supervised

The qualifications section should contain qualities you've learned that are beneficial for the position you're pursuing. Remember, employers want to know how the firm will benefit from hiring you. They're looking for someone who will fit the position. They want a person with some knowledge of the industry who will be aggressive about the job - a person of action. The following are a few examples:

QUALIFICATIONS:

As a trading assistant for one of the most successful silver traders on the NEW YORK COMMODITY EXCHANGE, learned the value of customer service and developed quantitative skills associated with securities analysis.

As a broker's assistant at MERRILL LYNCH, formed and honed cold calling skills, organized and maintained client accounts, reviewed for the Series 7 Exam.

As a student athlete, earned a reputation for honesty and integrity, demonstrated leadership and character, and acquired both interpersonal and quantitative skills.

QUALIFICATIONS:

As a management assistant for KMART, developed knowledge of the inventory control system and administered leadership duties in the supervision of employees.

As a management assistant at MON VALLEY COMMUNITY HOSPITAL, learned the value of dealing with a variety of people and administered bookkeeping services.

As a honor student, achieved success in academics through determination, dedication, and hard work.

List the qualifications section immediately after the objective for two reasons:

1) Experience is more relative to the position you're pursuing than which school you graduated from. Unless, however, you graduated from one of the nations top rated universities.

2) Listing education immediately under the objective will remind employers that you are a student, a candidate with little experience and qualifications. You don't want them to be reminded of that when they glance at your resume.

PROFESSIONAL EXPERIENCE

Don't list job details that don't relate to the position you're pursuing. They will take up valuable space and employers are only looking for details that will be useful for the position. For example, a job as a waitress will not help you land a marine biology position. Remember that you're trying to sell yourself, not take up space.

List anything you may have done in any position(s) you've held that relates to your objective. List it even if it was performed only once. You still gained experience from it.

Be proud of your professional experience(s). Give yourself a "catchy" professional sounding title that relates to your objective. For example, my summer position at Merrill Lynch didn't have a title. I listed my position as a *Broker's Assistant.* Immediately employers would realize that I gained quality experience that coincides with my objective.

Listing the dates of your job(s) is your discretion. While many believe dates are important, I disagree. Employers will see that they were internship experiences. Thus, they'll be reminded that you're a student. You don't want to provide any information that may cause them to draw a negative conclusion before you even get in the door for an interview. Be honest, but don't list anything that may be negative for you.

QUALIFICATIONS GAINED

The duties of your previous job(s) don't need to be listed. Employers are only concerned about what you've learned from your job(s) that will benefit the company.

Rather than duties, list a subheading called QUALIFICATIONS GAINED. Use impressive proactive words to describe the skills you've learned. Use such words as *learned, developed,* etc... (Refer to the list of proactive words on page 52) List two or three qualities learned for each job you're listing. Make sure they coincide with your objective so employers will be impressed when reading them.

The following are a few examples of how to state the professional experience and the qualifications gained sections.

PROFESSIONAL EXPERIENCE:

Trading
Assistant:

STEPHEN P. WILLNER
COMMODITY BROKERS
(New York City, NY)

Qualifications
Gained:

Administered client accounts for one of the most successful silver traders on the New York Commodity Exchange focusing on customer service and financial analysis.

Broker's
Assistant:

MERRILL LYNCH
(Hilo, Hawaii)

Qualifications
Gained:

Excelled at cold calling, maintained client accounts, progressed toward Series 7 license.

PROFESSIONAL EXPERIENCE:

Management
Assistant:

KMART

Qualifications
Gained:

Developed and organized the inventory control system for one of the nations largest companies.

Management
Assistant:

MON VALLEY
COMMUNITY HOSPITAL

Qualifications
Gained:

Supervised employees, organized and maintained the prescription inventory, and handled patient complaints.

EDUCATION

If you feel your education is more impressive than your professional experience then list it first under your objective. For example, if you're the Valedictorian of your class or if your Grade Point Average (GPA) is 4.0 then perhaps your education should be listed first. However, if you don't attend a well-known college, employers may not be as impressed with the honors. You want employers to develop a favorable opinion when reading about your educational background.

Unless your GPA is impressive, I wouldn't list it. My GPA was a 3.2 but I didn't feel it would impress employers. So I didn't include it on my resume.

If you've attended more than one college you should list them. Omitting a college can seem deceptive. Employers don't care if you've attended more than one college. The bottom line is that you've completed your college requirements and will be receiving a degree.

If you paid for your education by working, it could be beneficial to mention it. It will show that you worked hard for the education you've received. Employers will be impressed with your work ethic.

List any athletics you may have participated in for your college. Employers love to hire collegiate athletes because athletics teach leadership, competitiveness, and self discipline, as well as many other intangible qualities. These are the exact qualities most employers look for. Don't underestimate the influence that athletics has on employers. I know of many graduates who were hired mainly because of their athletic background.

The following is an example of how to list the education section:

EDUCATION:

UNIVERSITY OF HAWAII
Hilo, Hawaii

Bachelor of Business Administration
(Degree expected June 1996)

EDUCATION:

BOSTON UNIVERSITY
Boston, MA

Bachelor of Business Management
(Degree expected May 1996)

REFERENCES

You don't need to list names of actual references. And while many believe the phrase *References Available Upon Request* should be listed, I disagree. It takes up space and employers assume you can provide references if asked. One reason why you don't want to list references can be explained by the following example:

> Suppose you mail your resume to 100 different employers. You can conceivably have 100 employers, unexpectedly, calling your references. Your references may get upset by all of the calls, thus giving the employer negative feedback.

Another reason why you don't need to list references on your resume will be made evident by the technique suggested in chapter 8, *How To Separate Yourself From The Crowd.*

The following are examples of complete resumes with all parts grouped together. (They have been reduced to fit on the page)

ROBERT A. STEWART
4 Malia Street / Hilo, Hawaii 96720 / (808) 555-1212

OBJECTIVE: An entry level brokerage position with a retail investment firm that values superior sales ability, quality quantitative skills, and outstanding experience.

QUALIFICATIONS: As a trading assistant for one of the most successful silver traders
GAINED: on the **NEW YORK COMMODITY EXCHANGE,** learned the value of customer service and developed quantitative   skills associated with securities analysis.

As a broker's assistant at **MERRILL LYNCH,** formed and honed cold calling skills, organized and maintained client accounts, and reviewed for the Series 7 Exam.

As a student athlete, earned a reputation for honesty and integrity, demonstrated leadership and character, and acquired both interpersonal and quantitative skills.

PROFESSIONAL   Trading Assistant: **STEPHEN P. WILLNER COMMODITY**
EXPERIENCE: **BROKERS**   (New York City, NY)

Qualifications Gained: Administered client accounts for one of the most successful silver traders on the New York Commodity Exchange focusing on customer service and financial analysis.

Broker's Assistant: **MERRILL LYNCH** (Hilo, HI)

Qualifications Gained: Excelled   at   cold   calling, maintained   client   accounts, progressed   toward   Series   7 license.

EDUCATION: **UNIVERSITY OF HAWAII**   Hilo, Hawaii
(Bachelor of Business Administration)   (Degree expected June 1996)

Also attended University of Cincinnati and University of Pittsburgh

Qualifications Gained: Displayed leadership as a team captain and starting scholarshipped basketball player.

58

VICTORIA E. ANDERSON
1247 East Highland Avenue / Boston, MA 23176 / (987) 334-9876

OBJECTIVE: An entry level management position with a firm that values outstanding leadership, quality organizational skills, and extensive experience.

QUALIFICATIONS:
GAINED: As a management assistant for **KMART,** developed knowledge of the inventory control system and administered leadership duties in the supervision of employees.

As a management assistant at **MON VALLEY COMMUNITY HOSPITAL,** learned the value of dealing with a variety of patients and administered bookkeeping services.

As a honor student, achieved success in academics through determination, dedication, and hard work.

PROFESSIONAL
EXPERIENCE:

Management Assistant:	**KMART**
Qualifications Gained:	Developed and organized the inventory control system for one of the nations largest companies.
Management Assistant:	**MON VALLEY COMMUNITY HOSPITAL**
Qualifications Gained:	Supervised employees, organized and maintained the prescription inventory, and handled patient complaints.

EDUCATION: **BOSTON UNIVERSITY** Boston, MA
(Bachelor of Business Management) (Degree expected May 1996)

* **Academic Honor Roll every semester in college**
* **3.4 Grade Point Average**
* **Elected by peers as President of the Student Government**

ONE FINAL TIP ON RESUMES

As previously stated, there's no official way to write a resume. The resumes printed in this chapter are considered to be basic formats. It may be appropriate, however, to tailor your resume in an unique fashion for the position you're pursuing. For example, one recent graduate was seeking a position in the marketing or sales department of a recording company. To display his marketing talents he had his resume printed on the inside of a record album cover.

Another recent graduate was pursuing a marketing position for a large hotel chain, Hyatt. To be unique he printed his resume on bright pink neon paper. In addition, he had bright pink neon shirts and baseball hats printed with his name and the phrase, *Hyatt Hotels' Top Marketing Director!* He mailed the resume, shirt and hat to employers and was hired after the first interview.

Another recent graduate desired to work for a particular company in the wine industry. She took the initiative to find out that company's most popular selling wine. To separate herself from other candidates, she had her resume printed to fit on the bottle as a wine label and mailed it in a case to employers.

It's your discretion as to whether the basic resume format or an unique format is appropriate for the position you're pursuing. It's important to note that the more you can separate yourself in a professional manner from other candidates the better chance you'll have of standing out in the employers mind, which is exactly what you must try to accomplish.

CHAPTER 5

WRITING A COVER LETTER THAT SELLS YOU & YOUR RESUME

A cover letter must be sent with your resume. Its objective is to introduce you and interest the employer. It must be short but informative. As with the resume, the cover letter must sell you. Remember, your objective is to sell yourself to get an interview. You can sell yourself by drafting your cover letter in a sales letter format. A classic sales letter contains three paragraphs consisting of an introduction, body and closing.

INTRODUCTION

Never address your letter to the *Director of Personnel* or *To Whom It May Concern*. Make the effort to find out specifically who the appropriate person is by calling the company. Ask for the correct spelling of the person's name, title, and the company address. Misspelling any of these could cause your cover letter and resume to be thrown in the trash.

Begin the first paragraph by complimenting the employer. (This is a classic sales technique to help "win them over")

> Example: Dear Mr. Moffat,
>
> As a manager for one of the most successful retail investment firms,....
>
> Example: Dear Ms. Jones,
>
> As a leader for one of the most successful companies in the nation,...

This opening indirectly conveys respect for the employer and provides a positive first impression of the letter. Most people will continue reading a letter that begins by complimenting them.

The second part of the first sentence should tell employers what they need. Use successful, proactive words to describe the qualities they'd be looking for in candidates for the position you're pursuing.

Example: .....you are constantly looking for qualified, aggressive, and highly motivated salespeople to fill your sales force.

Example: .....you are constantly looking for qualified, organized, and highly motivated leaders to fill your management team.

Conclude the first paragraph by telling employers the qualities that will fulfill their need(s).

Example: These individuals not only need to be successful salespeople, but they need to possess excellent quantitative skills.

Example: These individuals not only need to be highly motivated, but they need to possess exceptional leadership ability.

The following are examples of the first paragraph with all parts grouped together.

Example: As a manager for one of the most successful retail investment firms, you are constantly looking for qualified, aggressive, and highly motivated salespeople to fill your sales force. These individuals not only need to be successful salespeople, but they need to possess excellent quantitative skills.

Example: As a leader for one of the most successful companies in the nation, you are constantly looking for qualified, organized, and highly motivated leaders to fill your management team. These individuals not only need to be highly motivated, but they need to possess exceptional leadership ability.

BODY

The second paragraph should tell employers that you possess the qualities to fulfill their need(s). Begin by telling them to review your resume. Then conclude by stating that you possess the qualities they're looking for in candidates pursuing that position. The following are examples of a complete second paragraph.

Please take the time to review the enclosed resume. You will clearly see that I have both quality sales experience and superior quantitative skills.

Please take the time to review the enclosed resume. You will clearly see that I have both quality management experience and exceptional leadership ability.

CLOSING

The final paragraph should begin by reiterating what you've said in the previous paragraphs, but with different words.

Example: Mr. Moffat, you need a high quality sales staff. One which excels at cold calling, demonstrates high quantitative skills, and is willing to take the initiative.

Example: Ms. Jones, you need a highly motivated management team. One which excels at motivating, demonstrates excellent organizational skills, and leads by example.

Again, use successful, proactive words to describe the qualities they'd like candidates to possess.

The second part of the final paragraph should show your desire for the position. Show employers you're willing to go out of your way to land the position. An excellent way to convey this is by stating that you'll be visiting their area *At Your Own Expense* or *Specifically To Meet With Them* during a certain period. This will convey that you're willing to go out of your way to interview.

Example: I will be visiting your area at my own expense from December 27, 19xx to January 7, 19xx.

Example: I will be in your area from December 27, 19xx to January 7, 19xx specifically to meet with you.

The final sentence of the last paragraph should be proactive. Don't ask employers for an interview. This will give them the opportunity to decline. You must "assume the appointment." In other words, tell employers you'll be calling them to arrange a convenient appointment. You will not call to ask for an appointment. You will call to schedule an appointment. There's a big difference. The latter shows that you're an aggressive, take charge type of person. Employers love candidates with these qualities.

Example: I will telephone you within one week to arrange a convenient appointment.

The following are examples of complete cover letters with all parts grouped together.

December 4, 19xx

Mr. Walter A. Moffat
Vice President
XYZ CORPORATION
456 Hickory Lane
Beverly Hills, CA 90210

Dear Mr. Moffat,

As a manager for one of the most successful retail investment firms, you are constantly looking for qualified, aggressive, and highly motivated salespeople to fill your sales force. These individuals not only need to be successful salespeople, but they need to possess excellent quantitative skills.

Please take the time to review the enclosed resume. You will clearly see that I have both quality sales experience and superior quantitative skills.

Mr. Moffat, you need a high quality sales staff. One which excels at cold calling, demonstrates high quantitative skills, and is willing to take the initiative. I will be visiting your area at my own expense from December 27, 19xx to January 7, 19xx. I will telephone you within one week to arrange a convenient appointment.

Sincerely,

Robert A. Stewart

VICTORIA E. ANDERSON

1247 East Highland Ave. / Boston, MA 23176 / (987) 334 9876

December 4, 19xx

Ms. Cindy J. Jones
Vice President
ABC CORPORATION
123 Albert Street
Boston, MA 23176

Dear Ms. Jones,

As a leader for one of the most successful companies in the nation, you are constantly looking for qualified, organized, and highly motivated leaders to fill your management team. These individuals not only need to be highly motivated, but they need to possess exceptional leadership ability.

Please take time to review the enclosed resume. You will clearly see that I have both quality management experience and exceptional leadership ability.

Ms. Jones, you need a highly motivated management team. One which excels at motivating, demonstrates excellent organizational skills, and leads by example. I will be in your area from December 27, 19xx to January 7, 19xx specifically to meet with you. I will telephone you within one week to arrange a convenient appointment.

Sincerely,

Victoria E. Anderson

The following are suggestions to remember for the cover letter and the envelope.

COVER LETTER SUGGESTIONS

1) Make sure to develop quality material. The cover letter is the initial contact with employers and will cause them to form a first impression of you.

2) The cover letter must flow with the resume. Consistent use of successful, proactive words is very important.

3) When grouping subjects together in one sentence the endings must agree. (Example: ed, ing)

4) Don't use the word "I" twice in the same sentence. It may cause employers to stall while reading. You want them to flow through the letter.

5) Use the same paper color, type face, and letter size that's used for the resume.

6) Use the same stationary format for your heading. This will convey a professional image.

7) The date, sincerely, and your name can be aligned on either the left column or in the center. I prefer centering. They are more visible.

8) Use a pen to crease the fold of your cover letter and resume. You want even the smallest detail to convey a professional image of you.

9) Don't fold the cover letter in the traditional way. Instead, do a reverse fold. This will allow your name to be showing constantly when the employer takes the letter out of the envelope and places it on the desk.

10) Send your resume and cover letter to employers approximately one month before you would like to interview. This will provide adequate time to follow up.

ENVELOPE SUGGESTIONS

1) The envelope must be the same quality of paper and color as your cover letter and resume.

2) Type the employer's address and your return address on the envelope. Typing in CAPITALS conveys a more powerful image.

3) Use a business type stamp if available. If not, use a conservative stamp such a *U.S. Flag* stamp. I used a Wall Street stamp on my envelopes to correspond with me seeking a position as a stockbroker. Never use a "love" stamp or a stamp with a person's picture on it. Every detail is important and employers notice details.

CHAPTER 6

HOW TO INTERVIEW
LIKE A PRO

The interview is the most crucial piece of your puzzle. This is when you must sell yourself in person. You don't have to convince the employers that you're the best qualified candidate for the position. You must only make them form the positive feeling that you would be a great asset to the company.

Remember, you will be competing against individuals more experienced, more qualified, and better suited for the position. It would be almost impossible for you to get hired solely on these criteria. You must make the employers feel so positive about you that they cannot pass on hiring you.

Instilling this positive gut feeling is much more important than being the best qualified. Employers may feel that even the most qualified candidate may not succeed in the firm's culture or in a particular position.

Many candidates were more experienced and more qualified than me. But I convinced my employer that I had the qualities necessary to be successful in the financial industry by making him form a positive gut feeling about me.

This is exactly what you must accomplish if you want to be hired. Every little detail about yourself is extremely important. Your fate can be decided, literally, in seconds. Some employers may rule out candidates based on their appearance. Others may do so after the initial handshake. You never know what makes employers dismiss the possibility of hiring a candidate. This is precisely why you must take notice of every detail.

The interview begins the second you enter the office. Other employees know when a potential candidate is present. They'll observe and form their own judgements. Employers will often ask employees for their impressions of candidates. Therefore, you must consistently convey a positive image from the very first moment you enter the office.

Start a conversation with the receptionist or secretary, asking questions about the company. This will show your interest and provide you with information that may help impress employers in the interview. Employers may even ask the receptionist or secretary for their impression of you. Thus, make sure you're courteous and friendly when speaking to them.

GET THE EMPLOYERS SECRETARY TO LIKE YOU

Most employers welcome and value their secretary's opinion of candidates. Some will even instruct their secretary to start a conversation with candidates before the interview to get a feel for the type of person they are when not on stage in front of the employer. You must get the secretary on your side. But how can you do this?

Here's a little technique that worked very well for me. I realized that when I would call an employer I would first have to speak with the secretary. I wanted to create a positive image that was unique and would stand out from other candidates. I decided to bring a small package of exotic coffee to each interview to give to each secretary. The following is an example as to how it was presented:

> *"I wanted to thank you for your kindness when I call for (The Employer). I brought a package of exotic coffee for you as a token of my sincere appreciation."*

The coffee made the secretary form a very positive impression of me and made me stand out from other candidates. I was the only candidate to present the secretary with a gift. From that moment on I was always remembered and spoken to in a polite manner when I telephoned. The secretary receives many calls for the employer. If I were to call and simply say:

> *"Hello, this is James Malinchak. May I speak with (The Employer)?"*

72

I probably wouldn't have been remembered. But when I called and said:

> *"Hello, this is James Malinchak. How did you enjoy your exotic coffee?"*

Immediately I was remembered. In addition, the secretary was always polite and made sure the employer took my call.

Giving the secretary a small gift is an excellent way to create a positive image for yourself and I highly recommend that you follow this technique. Bring a unique, but modest gift. Your intention is to stand out, not bribe.

Although employers make the final hiring decision, they realize that you'll need to work with current employees on a daily basis. Thus, employees impressions will surely be considered.

Employers seem to confide in their secretary more than other employees. What type of impression do you think you'll have made on their secretary if you give them a gift out of pure kindness?

Your main objective in the interview is to make the employer form a positive gut feeling about you. There are two criteria to keep in mind to accomplish this:

1)   FIRST IMPRESSIONS

2)   HOW TO SPEAK TO EMPLOYERS

1)   <u>FIRST IMPRESSIONS</u>

As you're already aware, *Perception is Reality.* Employers prejudge candidates within the first few minutes of meeting them. As unfair as it may be, it's very true.

You must do everything possible to make a positive impact on the initial contact. Remember, *You Never Get a Second Chance To Make A Positive First Impression*. But how can you make employers form this positive impression of you upon the initial meeting? The following will help you to do so.

DRESS

Dress with the intent of relaying a professional and powerful image. It may cost you a little money to do so, but it will be money well spent. Don't go overboard. Spend only what you can afford.

Dressing informally will not convey a positive impression. Dressing like an experienced business professional will. You must *look the role*. Remember, *Perception Is Reality*. The following will help you to convey these images.

PROFESSIONAL

To dress in a professional manner, you must blend with the people who are currently working in that industry. Determine the styles of the industry then simply adopt those styles.

When I began searching for the style(s) of the brokerage industry, I simply observed what *successful* brokers were wearing. I even asked a few what they recommended. Generally, a suit for men and a dress or pants suit for women.

POWERFUL

Dress in dark colors to convey a powerful image. Employers associate dark colored clothing with a powerful personality. A candidate sporting dark colored clothing is *perceived* to be a strong, powerful, and aggressive person who is self-confident. Wear conservative clothing which contains dark blue, black, brown, burgundy, or red colors.

Make sure to take notice of every article of your outfit. If you're a male, coordinate your tie, belt, shoes, and socks. Your shirt should be plain white and a red tie is recommended. If you're a female, coordinate your shoes, blouse, and dress or skirt.

CONVEY CONFIDENCE

Confidence will convey to employers that you have the ability to overcome objections and obstacles as they arise. If you don't convey confidence in yourself during the interview employers will be uncertain about your ability and it's unlikely you'll be hired. The following will help you to convey confidence.

HOLD YOUR HEAD HIGH

A person whose chin is down conveys a timid, insecure image. This person will likely fail when met with objection. Employers want employees who possess strength and stability when confronted with obstacles. Holding your head high will help to convey this message.

POWERFUL HANDSHAKE

It's essential for you to shake the employers hand firmly. A firm handshake will convey that you believe in yourself and your ability. A former Vice President of a Fortune 500 company once told me that if a candidate came into an interview and didn't shake his hand firmly the candidate wouldn't be hired. He didn't care how qualified or suitable the candidate was. The handshake told him if candidates had confidence in their ability to perform the job.

EYE CONTACT

You must always look employers in the eye when speaking and listening to them. Eye contact conveys confidence and tells employers you're very interested in what they're telling you. Try not to lose eye contact, but don't get in a staring contest.

You may think these suggestions aren't important. But remember, it only matters what employers think. Unfortunately, you may never know what will cause employers to dismiss a candidate from consideration for a position.

2)   HOW TO SPEAK TO EMPLOYERS

Many employers believe that the way you speak to them is the way you'll speak to customers and clients. Therefore, it's essential for you to impress employers with what you say.

You've probably had an experience where you were interested in a person until you heard them speak. It's the same for employers. They may like what they visually perceive about you. But if you don't speak in a confident and professional manner they may not hire you.

The following will help you convey a more positive impression to employers during the interview.

THINK BEFORE YOU SPEAK

This is probably the most important suggestion you'll need to know. How many times have you said something that, later, you wished was never said? When answering a question or commenting, ask yourself if your response might cause the employer to form a negative impression of you. If you think it's possible, then absolutely don't say it.

BELIEVE IN WHAT YOU SAY

The worst thing you can do during the interview is to put on an act or try to fool the employer. If you don't believe in what you're saying the employer will sense it. Convey your comments with sincerity.

ALWAYS SPEAK POSITIVE

Employers love a positive attitude. Think about it. If you were an employer would you want your customers, clients, and other employees interacting with an employee who spoke in a negative manner? Everything that you say must be positive when speaking to the employer. Even if a negative situation arises find something positive to say about it.

USE SIR OR MA'AM

Address the employer as Sir or Ma'am. For example, *Thank you for meeting with me Sir,* or *It's a pleasure meeting you Ma'am.* People love to be addressed in this manner because it conveys respect. Remember, employers feel you'll address customers and clients in the same manner in which you address them.

SPEAK CLEARLY AND ARTICULATELY

Use proper English (no slang) when speaking and avoid running words together. Don't ruin your chances of being hired because of speaking incorrectly. The following are a few examples.

Do Not Say	Do Say
I been	I have been
Oughta	Ought to or Should
I ain't / It ain't	I am not / It is not
Yah	Yes

Not pronouncing words properly will make you sound unprofessional. Remember, employers *perceive* that you will speak to customers and clients in the same manner.

A good exercise is to have someone tell you when you are running words together or omitting letters. Write those words down and practice pronouncing them correctly. You'll be surprised at how your articulation will improve.

ANSWERING INTERVIEW QUESTIONS

Employers will ask you many questions. Your answers must be direct, confident, intelligent, and to the point. Don't give long, drawn out answers. You're trying to sell yourself, not bore the employer.

Practice answering the possible questions employers may ask. Use a tape recorder to hear if you're speaking clearly and articulating properly. The following is a list of questions that may be asked by employers.

- Why did you choose this field of work?
- Why would you like to work for this company?
- What do you know about our company?
- Why should we hire you?
- What sets you apart from other candidates who want this position?
- Why do you think you'd succeed at this job?
- What are your major strengths? Weaknesses?
- What is your most significant achievement?
- What are you most proud of in your life?
- What have you done that shows initiative?
- What was the biggest challenge you've ever faced?
- What was the biggest obstacle you've ever overcome?
- What kind of people do you like? Dislike?
- Where do you see yourself in five years?
- What are your career goals?
- How are you going to achieve your career goals?

These are some of the more common questions you may be asked. I was asked every one of them during my interviews. You may also be asked questions about college courses and activities, work experience, and the specific position you're applying for.

QUESTIONS YOU MIGHT ASK

To have a positive and effective interview you must ask appropriate questions. Again, preparation is the key. Think of questions that are tailored to the position you're pursuing or the company. Make a list of the questions to take with you. Employers will be impressed if you refer to the list during the interview. It will show that you're serious about the position.

The following suggestions are questions you may want to ask:

- What will my duties/responsibilities be?
- Who would I report to? What's his/her background?
- Who are the other people I'd report to? What are their backgrounds?
- Do you provide on-going training for employees?
- What kind of equipment will I be using?
- Are there performance reviews?
- What future positions could I advance toward?
- What are the company's strengths? Weaknesses?

(Questions to Learn About the Employer)
- How long have you been with the company? In the industry?
- How did you land your position with the company?
- What do you like most about your job/industry? Least?
- What are your goals for the company? Your department?
- Who are your most successful employees?
- What characteristics do you notice that separates them from other employees?
- What kind of person are you looking for?

The last question is an excellent question to ask. It will reveal the exact qualities the employer is looking for in candidates. It will then be your job to convince the employer that you possess these qualities.

The majority of the above questions were asked by me in my interviews. However, they're only suggestions. You may want to formulate your own.

Most employers will ask you to describe your strengths and weaknesses. Stating your strengths is easy. State those positive qualities that they're looking for. For example, any employer will love a candidate who is:

- Motivated	- Competitive
- Focused	- Organized
- Hard Working	- Driven By Success
- Goal Oriented	- A Winner
- Tenacious	- A Leader

You may think that stating your weaknesses may not be as easy. You're right. It's a catch 22 situation. You don't want to say anything that may hurt your chances of being hired. However, employers may feel deceived if you say that you don't have any weaknesses. So what should you say?

Briefly state a weakness. Then overshadow it with positive qualities. The following is an example:

"You may think my age is a weakness. But what I may lack in age I certainly make up for with aggressiveness, competitiveness, and a desire to succeed."

By focusing the employer's attention on the positive qualities you can turn what seems to be a negative into a positive situation.

INTERVIEW SUGGESTIONS

The following are suggestions to remember when preparing for the interview.

1) <u>LEARN ABOUT THE COMPANY</u>: You may be asked questions about the company, a specific department, or the position. Impress employers with your company knowledge.

2) <u>BE CONFIDENT</u>: Don't think less of your abilities because of your age, lack of qualifications or lack of experience. If you're confident that you can do the job then convey it during the interview.

3) <u>ARRIVE EARLY</u>: Most people say you should arrive 15 minutes before the interview. However, I believe you should arrive at least one hour before so you can practice. Review your answers to the questions the employer may ask. Remember, preparation is the key.

4) <u>DON'T SLOUCH</u>: Sit up straight with your chin up. (Just like a marine.) Slouching may lead employers to think that you're sloppy and unorganized.

5) <u>KEEP YOUR COMPOSURE AT ALL TIMES</u>: Employers may test you with certain comments or questions to see how you react under pressure. Stay calm, take a deep breath, and answer in a composed and thoughtful manner.

6) <u>COMPLIMENT THE EMPLOYER</u>: People appreciate honest and sincere praise. Learn something positive that the employer is doing within the company and compliment him/her on it. *Flattery Will Get You Everywhere.*

7) <u>LEARN THE EMPLOYERS PERSONAL INTEREST(S)</u>: Find an interest that you and the employer have in common and start a conversation about it. *People Like People Who Are Like Themselves.* Observe things in the employer's office as you first enter. Indications of their interest(s) will usually be on display.

8) <u>NO FLASHY JEWELRY</u>: A student can rarely afford an expensive piece of jewelry. Look professional, not fake. Employers first impressions of you are crucial. Don't give them the impression that you're fake.

9) <u>BE AWARE OF EXAMS</u>: Don't panic if asked to take an exam. This is a positive sign. Employers will only test those candidates in which they are truly interested. Personality exams are the most common. Most employers want to know what type of person they're considering hiring.

10) <u>THINK OF HOW YOU WILL BENEFIT THE EMPLOYER</u>: Employers only care about the company. Think of how the company will benefit from hiring you and convey this during the interview.

11) <u>INTERVIEW APPROXIMATELY 6 MONTHS BEFORE GRADUATION</u>: Most students don't interview until after graduation. This is a big mistake! Interviewing approximately 6 months before graduation will give you an advantage over those not interviewing until after graduation. Also, it will make a positive impression on employers.

12) <u>PRACTICE MAKES PERFECT</u>: If you don't practice before your interview, you may have a poor meeting. Practice both in the mirror and on a tape recorder. Practice your articulation, grammar, eye contact, posture, etc.....

CHAPTER 7

FOLLOWING UP IN A PROFESSIONAL AND UNIQUE MANNER

After the interview, it's essential to follow up with employers. It's highly unlikely you'll be hired if you don't have the consideration to thank employers for their time. They took time out of their busy schedules to meet with you and you should show your appreciation.

Send a thank you letter immediately following the interview. The letter should be short and should mention the date of your interview. Use the same type face, letter size, heading, and the exact paper used for your resume and cover letter. Using the same stationary will allow you to continue to convey a professional image. A professional image is very important when pursuing any position.

BE UNIQUE

Employers may interview many candidates and may not remember you when your thank you letter arrives. You need to separate yourself from other candidates. But how can you do this?

I separated myself from other candidates by sending a small gift with my letter. Employers receive many thank you letters after interviews. But very few, if any, will be accompanied by a gift.

My gift was exotic coffee. The exact same exotic coffee that I presented to their secretary before the interview. (Notice the connection?) The coffee not only made me stand out in the employers mind, but it also made them remember me when I made a follow up phone call. When they answered the call I would simply say:

"Good morning Mr/Mrs (Employer). This is James Malinchak. How did you enjoy the exotic coffee I sent you?"

Although they may not have remembered me when I said my name, they surely knew who I was when I mentioned the coffee. Most of the employers were very grateful for the coffee and some even commented that their wife/husband also enjoyed it. (Talk about "brownie points!")

84

In addition to sending a thank you letter and gift to employers, you should also do so for their secretary. Thank them for being so helpful and kind during your visit. They'll surely mention the letter to the employers, which will only lead them to form a more positive image of you.

The following are examples of thank you letters that can be mailed to employers and their secretary.

ROBERT A. STEWART
4 Malia Street / Hilo, HI 96720 / (808) 555-1212

January 6, 19xx

Mr. Walter A. Moffat
Vice President
XYZ CORPORATION
456 Hickory Lane
Beverly Hills, CA 90210

Dear Mr. Moffat,

I wanted to thank you for taking the time to meet with me on December 30th. Please accept this package of exotic coffee as a token of my sincere appreciation.

As I stated in our meeting, my goal is to be employed with your firm. I will telephone you within one week to discuss my situation further.

Thank you for your time and best wishes.

Sincerely,

Robert A. Stewart

January 6, 19xx

Ms. Betty Szabo
XYZ CORPORATION
456 Hickory Lane
Beverly Hills, CA 90210

Dear Betty,

I wanted to, again, thank you for your kindness on the telephone and when I visited your office. Please accept this exotic coffee as a token of my sincere appreciation.

Thank you, Betty, and best wishes.

Sincerely,

Robert A. Stewart

TELEPHONE FOLLOW UP

About one week after sending the thank you letter and gift, make a follow up call to the employer. The purpose of the call is to thank the employer, again, for the interview and to express your continued interest in the position. The call should be brief and to the point. Make sure to mention to both the secretary and employer the small gift that accompanied your thank you letters.

If the hiring decision will not be made for a certain period of time, you should call the employer periodically. Call every two or three weeks just to remain in contact. This will demonstrate your desire for the position. The more you speak to the employers and their secretaries the better the relationships you will build.

LETTER FOLLOW UP

Approximately every two or three weeks send the employer a letter to reinforce the fact that you want the position. Each letter must state indirectly that you're the best person for the position. When writing these letters, refer to the qualities mentioned in chapter one that most employers look for in candidates.

State in your letters that you possess these positive qualities and that they need an individual with these qualities working for them. Remember, employers only care about how you can benefit the company.

These letters will be an important part of your job pursuit. The more you can get your name in front of employers in a positive manner the more familiar they'll become with you and your background.

The following are examples of the type of motivating letters to send to employers on a continuous basis. Feel free to use them or adapt them for your individual situation. (Note: I mailed these exact letters during the pursuit of my job.)

February 14, 19xx

Mr. Walter A. Moffat
Vice President
XYZ CORPORATION
456 Hickory Lane
Beverly Hills, CA 90210

Dear Mr. Moffat,

I am a firm believer in helping people to achieve their needs and desires. Even if I am under no-obligation to help them. I term this action as "GOING THE EXTRA MILE" and my philosophy for it is simple: If you go the extra mile to help people, it will pay off for you in the long-run.

This is exactly how I will conduct business for your firm; "GOING THE EXTRA MILE" to help clients achieve their needs and desires.

Sincerely,

Robert A. Stewart

ROBERT A. STEWART
4 Malia Street / Hilo, HI 96720 / (808) 555-1212

March 14, 19xx

Mr. Walter A. Moffat
Vice President
XYZ CORPORATION
456 Hickory Lane
Beverly Hills, CA 90210

Dear Mr. Moffat,

I am a diligent, hard working individual who would be an asset to your firm. I am an extremely goal oriented person who is a firm believer that "hard work pays off."

I have used this cliche' throughout my entire life and it has allowed me to achieve my goals. I know what it takes, not only to compete, but to WIN! These qualities are not instilled within every individual that interviews with you for a position. You would be allowing a highly successful person to "slip" away by not offering me a position with your firm.

Sincerely,

Robert A. Stewart

ROBERT A. STEWART
4 Malia Street / Hilo, HI 96720 / (808) 555-1212

April 14, 19xx

Mr. Walter A. Moffat
Vice President
XYZ CORPORATION
456 Hickory Lane
Beverly Hills, CA 90210

Dear Mr. Moffat,

Have you ever wanted something badly enough that you could almost taste it? Your mind is constantly filled with thoughts of this one goal. Your heart continuously feels a burning desire. Your energy level is always operating at full capacity.

This happens when I think about landing a position with your firm!

Mr. Moffat, my goal is to be employed with your firm and my abilities *should not* be taken lightly. You will not find many people with my discipline, tenacity, or determination.

Sincerely,

Robert A. Stewart

Employers love candidates who are assertive and persistent. To get the position, you must do more than the other candidates; YOU MUST GO THE EXTRA MILE!

Don't forget the fact that other candidates may be more experienced, more qualified, and older. Go out of your way to prove that you desire the position more. Be persistent and consistent in your approach but don't be obnoxious. Don't contact the employer every few days. You don't want to convey the impression that you're a pest.

Following up with consistency will demonstrate your professionalism and your ability to complete a task. These are qualities that every employer would love for their employees to possess.

CHAPTER 8

HOW TO SEPARATE YOURSELF FROM THE CROWD

You may feel very positive about the interviews you've conducted. Hopefully you'll have sold the employers on you by conveying that you're much too valuable for them not to offer you a position. And that's exactly what your objective should be for every interview.

No matter how well the interview may have gone there will still be that one terrible negative that continues to haunt you; you're probably competing against candidates who are more experienced and more qualified. If they are more experienced and more qualified then they probably have more references as well.

If you were an employer who would you feel more comfortable hiring: The student with a few references or the more experienced and qualified individual who probably has more references than you can count on one hand? I'm quite certain we both agree the student would be ruled out. If you don't overcome this obstacle you can be eliminated from consideration.

I was faced with the same predicament. I sold my positive qualities during the interviews. However, it just didn't seem to be enough to propel me above the competition. I realized that the opportunity of landing the job I desired might slip away if I didn't overcome this obstacle.

I spoke with a few local employers to find out if a candidate's references were contacted during the interview process. Surprisingly, every employer agreed that references weren't usually contacted after the initial interview.

Immediately, an idea flashed through my mind. What if various successful individuals sent recommendation letters on my behalf? I was sure this was an unique idea that would get me noticed and help to build my credibility.

I firmly believe these letters *put the icing on the cake* for me. As I periodically called the employers to express my continued interest in the position, they began mentioning the letters. One employer commented, "I have never received so many letters in support of one individual. You must be well respected among your peers." After hearing this statement I knew that my chances of being hired had increased tremendously.

I strongly recommend that you follow this technique. It's an excellent way for you to have your name in front of employers on a continuous basis.

Receiving recommendation letters from successful individuals with impressive career titles (that's the key) will help convince employers that you're well respected by various Real World professionals. In addition, employers will see that you're GOING THE EXTRA MILE to pursue the position. Your effort will surely impress employers and allow you to stand out from other candidates.

Make a list of various successful professionals that you know who will make a positive impression on employers and ask them for their support. Some of the people you may want to ask are your professors, your internship employer(s), your priest, college and professional athletic coaches, doctors, lawyers, politicians, the Chief of Police, people working for large well-known corporations, any celebrities or professional athletes, and especially anyone who is successful in the profession in which you're pursuing a job. Basically, you want anyone who might impress employers. I've never met one person who was not willing to write a recommendation letter to help a friend.

Ask each person to type the letter on their professional stationary so it makes a favorable impression. Remember, PERCEPTION IS REALITY! You must make employers perceive that you're a well respected individual in the Real World.

Many qualified individuals have not been hired because their competitors knew more influential people. Remember, employers have one thought in mind when considering possible candidates: What can this person do for the firm? If they receive recommendation letters on your behalf and *perceive* that you'll benefit the firm, partly because of your contacts, then your chances of being hired will increase tremendously.

The following are a few of the recommendation letters that were sent on my behalf. They're not printed to impress you. I'm merely providing examples of the type of letters you may want to have written about you.

Dear ....

A decade ago, I was a successful account executive for a major brokerage firm. As such, I understand your need to maintain an effective, ethical sales staff. You need intelligent, motivated and competent employees to help your office increase its sales production. For these goals, the best employment decision you can make this year is to hire James R. Malinchak.

Yes, this is another letter endorsing James Malinchak as a broker trainee for your office. As you can tell, James has *sold* many knowledgeable people on his ability and integrity. I am convinced James will be a top producer for the brokerage firm wise enough to hire him. I was a quality producer for my firm (number one on the production lists on several occasions) and I am convinced James will be a better producer than me.

I am *sold* on James Malinchak. He has integrity, ability and tenacity. He will be a valuable addition to your production staff. It is important you hire him now and train him well. This will be one of the best employment decisions you will ever make.

Sincerely,

William E. Wilson, PhD
Assistant Professor of Finance

Dear ....

I am writing to you and other executives of your organization to present a recommendation for Mr. James Malinchak. He is my student at the University of Hawaii in the School of Business, and one of our outstanding graduates.

Mr. Malinchak has expressed a great deal of interest in your firm, and particularly in your location. I am impressed by his focused intention and specific knowledge about your company. When a person as dedicated as this gentleman is to his work at the university expresses such particular regard and desire to become part of an organization, I believe his initiative and qualities should be brought to your attention.

As an educator now, but recently retired as Vice President of Sales and Marketing for Allied Signal Aerospace Canada, I have had substantial experience in identifying people of high success potential. Without reservation, Mr. Malinchak's abilities and initiative are indicative of a special achievement quality that I believe will serve your firm well.

I am pleased to offer this recommendation that you employ Mr. Malinchak. If you have any questions in regard to my statement, Please call. Thank you.

Sincerely,

Dr. Robert L. Polk

CHAPTER 9

PERSISTENCE IS THE KEY THAT CAN UNLOCK MANY DOORS

Many people believe that talent, industry knowledge, or higher education is what allows certain individuals to be hired over others. But I know of many people who possess these qualities and are still unemployed or working at a job that is below their capabilities.

I was not hired at Merrill Lynch over other candidates because of my superior sales talents or financial knowledge. I didn't have extensive experience because I was still completing my final year of college. And, although I did take college finance courses, I only had minimum financial knowledge.

In addition, I was not hired because I graduated from one of the nations top rated business schools. My diploma did not read Harvard or Yale.

I knew that not possessing these qualities could possibly eliminate my chances of being hired. After all, what did I have to offer a company like Merrill Lynch?

I began thinking of how to overcome what seemed to be an enormous obstacle. Again, how could I possibly compete against candidates who possessed any, or all, of these qualities? In reality I couldn't. Employers probably would not have even taken me seriously. Day after day I continuously racked my brain trying to find a way around this obstacle.

One day as I was reading a book, I came across a quotation that provided the answer I had been searching for:

> *"Nothing in the world can take the place of persistence. Talent will not; nothing is more common than unsuccessful men with talent. Genius will not; unrewarded genius is almost a proverb. Education will not; the world is full of educated derelicts. Persistence and determination alone are omnipotent."*
>
> -CALVIN COOLIDGE

Without a doubt, persistence was the key that got me hired. There were many candidates more qualified and more experienced, but none were more persistent.

Employers love persistent candidates. Dr. Robert Polk, a retired Vice President of Sales and Marketing for Allied Signal Aerospace Canada, reinforced my notion that persistence is the key. I remember Dr. Polk telling me that he believed the most important thing for an individual to do when pursuing a position is to be persistent. He told me a story of a young graduate who contacted him on a continuous basis for over six months asking to be hired. Dr. Polk said,

> *"This girl would not give up. I told her numerous times that we didn't have a position for her but she just wouldn't take no for an answer. I was so impressed with her persistence that I offered her the first position that came available. Her persistence showed me that she desired to be hired more than any other candidate. I was not about to let a person like her slip through my fingers."*

When I began working at Merrill Lynch, a Financial Consultant named Ron Visconti said to me,

> *"You would've never been hired at Merrill Lynch had you not been so aggressive and persistent."*

Mr. Visconti is a Vice President who has been with Merrill Lynch for approximately 20 years. In addition, he's a former office manager who frequently hired candidates. When I heard a person of his background and experience say this, I knew my idea of being persistent is key when pursuing any position.

Landing the job you truly desire right out of college will not be easy. You may have to persist for a period of time. That's generally how successful people in the Real World achieve success; by being persistent in the pursuit of their goals.

Success doesn't come easily or just happen to people. The CEO of Kmart didn't land his top position because he showed up to work everyday and they kept promoting him. Bill Clinton didn't become President of the United States just because he went to law school. Michael Jordan didn't become the greatest basketball player to play the game just because he decided to put on a pair of NIKE shoes.

Success doesn't happen that way. It happens by overcoming obstacles and adversity while persisting in a positive manner toward your goals.

Don't get discouraged or quit if you don't land the position you desire immediately. Thomas Edison invented the light bulb after approximately 25,000 unsuccessful attempts. Abraham Lincoln lost approximately 7 elections before becoming President of the United States. Michael Jordan was once cut from his high school basketball team. I was rejected by many employers before finally getting hired. Don't worry about the discouragement when pursuing your job. The only way you can fail is if you quit and give up.

> *"Many of life's failures are men who did not realize how close they were to success when they gave up."*

> -UNKNOWN

You will face objections and rejections in the pursuit of your job. Realize this because it's just a part of the job hunt. These are the exact obstacles discussed in chapter one that you *must* overcome. Don't give up when you're faced with one of these roadblocks. If you truly desire a certain position don't quit until you land it. Be persistent and don't take no for an answer. Eventually employers will realize that your desire for the position is stronger than that of any other candidates. It will be then that the door to the position you desire will be opened.....

> *"Knock on the door of the place where you want to work, frequently and firmly, and eventually someone will let you in........."*

> -UNKNOWN

CHAPTER 10

TIPS
FROM EMPLOYERS
ABOUT GETTING
HIRED

An old cliche' states, *Knowledge Is Power!* The more you know about a subject the more of an advantage you'll have in achieving your goal. The same holds true when pursuing any job. The more information you can gather about what certain employers look for the better the chance that you'll be hired.

I thought a great way to end this book would be to have various employers comment and offer advice that will help you in your job pursuit. These are successful professionals who have reviewed numerous candidates. Their comments will provide you with a better understanding of what employers look for when searching for potential employees. Each individual was asked to elaborate on the same five questions. Their responses have been structured in a basic question and answer format to allow for easy reading.

RON VISCONTI
Vice President and Former Resident Manager
MERRILL LYNCH

1.   <u>What do you look for in candidates</u>?

> *"I look for three things. Number one is appearance. That goes for everything from top to bottom. Not only clothes but your hair, fingernails and also how you present yourself.*
>
> *Number two is enthusiasm. Is the person excited about working for me and the company?*
>
> *Thirdly, I want someone who has the ability to assemble ideas and arguments into a single vision and then be able to communicate that vision to everyone from the smartest person to the least smartest person. They need to be able to think for themselves with common sense."*

2.   <u>How important are internships</u>?

> *"Internships are extremely important. Nothing beats*

experience. All the education in the world doesn't measure experience. Internships allow you to learn something about the field you're interested in and enable you to find out if you really want to pursue that career.

Good grades are important but if I had two candidates of equal capabilities, one with straight A's but no internship experience and the other with C's but internship experience I'd take the C student in a heartbeat."

3. <u>How should the soon-to-be graduate interview</u>?

"You have to take pride in your appearance. Everything from your hair to your fingernails is important. Take notice of every detail and make sure your shoes are shined. I look at every detail. You don't get a second chance to make a good first impression.

Be aware of your mannerisms. Give a good firm handshake and look me in the eye. Don't come into an interview weak. That tells me that the Real World will chew you up and spit you out.

You need to have a self-assured attitude. Display confidence, common sense, and the ability to be cordial. I don't look for someone with a lot of knowledge about the industry because we're going to train you. But it's important for you to display those other qualities."

4. <u>How can a soon-to-be graduate actually compete against and get hired over more experienced and more qualified candidates</u>?

"You have to be persistent. Persistence pays off. In addition, be willing to accept any position that's available in order to get your foot in the door. Once you get in the door do things that will allow you to shine. One way you can always shine is by doing the extra, whatever that involves. Go the extra

mile, don't just do the job at hand. No matter where you are in the company if you don't shine you don't get ahead. And actions speak louder than words.

There are stairs leading up the pyramid and you have to be willing to climb them, sometimes starting at the bottom. Every step along the way you have to make sure that you're a shining star no matter what others may say. You must stand out over and above everyone else."

5. <u>What advice would you give to the soon-to-be graduate about to enter the Real World</u>?

"You've lost your umbrella of mom and dad. Now you have to take responsibility for your actions. All you have to look forward to is 40 years of work. Life revolves around your career. Whether you think it does or not, it does. So choose a career you'll enjoy doing in an area you'll enjoy living. Ask yourself the following questions:

> *-Is this what I want to do for the rest of my life?*
> *-Is there any chance for upward mobility in the company?*
> *-Is there continuing education within the company?*
> *-Is my degree enough to carry me through life or will I need an MBA or PhD?*

Remember, your degree is only your ticket to ride. It just gets you on the train, it doesn't guarantee your destination."

DAVY J. TYBURSKI
General Manager
KINETIC CONCEPTS, INC. (KCI)

1. <u>What do you look for in candidates</u>?

"There are three key points that I look for. First would be the appearance of the person, in general. Are they clean-cut?

Do they dress well? Everything that goes with appearance.

The second thing, obviously, would be confidence in themselves and I think there's a fine line between confidence and being cocky. The type of person that when I'm chatting with them I know they're comfortable with themselves. If they're comfortable with themselves then they'll represent my company well because they'll be comfortable with the company.

Thirdly, and I think the most important, is a positive attitude. Usually with anyone I speak with, within the first two minutes I can tell what their outlook on life is. It's either positive or negative. And I feel the most important thing to look for when considering a candidate is if they have a positive attitude because then, it's an I can do, I will do, I want to do type person as compared to someone who tries to find an excuse as to why they're not getting something done by a certain deadline or maybe always finding excuses as to why they didn't complete a task."

2. <u>How important are internships</u>?

"Obviously if there were two candidates and one did an internship with an organization and one didn't do an internship I would have to give an extra point to the person who did the internship for a few reasons:

Number one, they've already had a real life experience of what a working organization is like. The second thing would be is that they've already worked in a career. Going to school, graduating, and going into the job market is completely different as compared to someone who already has a period of time that they've actually been trained and had some real life experience(s) on the job as an intern. And I think that's real important just because of the real life experience of doing something as compared to just working in a text book."

3.   How should the soon-to-be graduate interview?

"You need to research the company that you're interviewing with and really have a good understanding of what the company does before you walk into the interview. Also, be prepared in case the employer asks, what can you do for me and for the company? If you've already researched the company and you know that, for example, the past year hasn't been a good year for them for whatever reason, you may be able to present some new and enlightening ideas to the person who's interviewing you. I think it will give you a big advantage because it shows employers that, not only did you take the time to research the company, but also that you're using your mind to develop solutions."

4.   How can a soon-to-be graduate actually compete against and get hired over more experienced and more qualified candidates?

"There are two things that go with this question. Number one, from a profitability standpoint an employer may look at a recent college graduate first as compared to someone who has 5, 10, or 15 years of experience in the field for one major reason. I can hire a recent graduate for a lot less money than I can hire someone who has ten years of experience.

The second thing is, you've got to remember that most seasoned professionals have a good working knowledge of what they need to do. But also they have some bad habits. The positive thing with a recent graduate is that they're fresh and they don't have a long history of building bad habits so I'd be able to train that person the way that I'd want them to function. It's kind of like a new baby, so to speak. You teach them the habits that you want them to learn and they don't have those bad habits built in.

As to why I would consider hiring a recent graduate over a seasoned professional is that, in my heart, if I feel that

107

someone can do a great job for me even though they have no experience then I'd hire them. If they have the right attitude, are comfortable with themself, and if they present themself well to me then I know they're going to present themselves well to my customers."

5.   <u>What advice would you give to the soon-to-be graduate about to enter the Real World</u>?

"The first thing is really basic but I don't think that a lot of people think about it. It's having a specific, laid-out plan of what they really want to do. I remember when I was graduating I would ask others what they were going to do after graduation and they weren't really sure. That's the problem with a lot of college students. They go to school and they say they're going to get a great job when they graduate. But if you ask them what that job is, who's it with, how much does it pay, where they're going to be living, etc... they have no idea. You need to have clear guidelines of what to expect. If you're not clear on what you want to do then you're going to be wasting a lot of your time looking in all different areas of the employment world without really having a clear focus.

The second thing that you need is persistence. You can't give up. And you should start the process of looking for a career months before you graduate. Don't wait till the last minute. Don't wait till you wake up one day, and you've graduated and you decide, well, it's time to go get a job. You've got to give yourself at least four to six months before something's going to happen. Also, I think you put a lot of pressure on yourself if you wait till the last minute. It's the same as a homework assignment. You don't start working on a huge term paper the night before. You work on a little every night so that when it's time to be turned in, you feel comfortable with what you've done."

DR. ROBERT L. POLK
Retired Vice President of Sales and Marketing
ALLIED SIGNAL AEROSPACE CANADA

1. What do you look for in candidates?

"The first thing I look for is a pleasing personality. Without that, there's no reason to go much further. The organization contribution will be better received and more effective with a harmonious manner.

The next thing is to see if they have some resourcefulness in addition to their education. This is a process of inquiry about their knowledge of my firm. That is, do they have some general knowledge about our firm and our industry; or better yet, some experience in it?

The last thing I look for is the type of references furnished. My interest here is whether there is representation by an industry member I might know. Although such a reference could certainly be a plus in the candidate's favor, my real concern is whether there is a solid work ethic reference."

2. How important are internships?

"I consider internships to be reasonably important, although not mandatory. The reason is that it exhibits a higher than usual potential interest in the business, as well as a general understanding of the firm that would otherwise require possibly a considerable orientation investment on our part."

3. How should the soon-to-be graduate interview?

"The main thing I would advise people to do is to prepare by investing time in learning some facts about the firm, the general industry, and if possible, about the person they will be interviewing with. This exhibits both initiative and higher than average interest in getting the job; an indication to me

of higher potential for future success."

4.   How can a soon-to-be graduate actually compete against and get hired over more experienced and more qualified candidates?

"I think it depends upon how much energy you expend in going after the job. Industriousness and initiative can count for more than experience when coupled with enthusiasm and interest. These factors can indicate potential to contribute as a result of willingness to learn and desire to become part of the organization."

5.   What advice would you give the soon-to-be graduate about to enter the Real World?

"The organization is made up of many different people, from janitors, to secretaries, to your future peers, and management. The company's success depends on how well they perform their different duties. But it also depends on other contributions like ideas about how to make the firm better in some respect. I suggest adopting a listening and learning attitude that recognizes the importance of everyone in the company, so that as you move up in the firm, you will do so with the respect of others."

NICK JEMO
Operations Manager
KMART

1.   What do you look for in candidates?

"Attitude is a big part of what I look for. A lot of the skills that a candidate needs will be learned on the job. The knowledge that you gain in college is very important but if you have the attitude and drive to go out and learn what we need you to learn then you will succeed. Attitude and drive is such a big part of it."

2.   How important are internships?

"Speaking from my personal experience, I did not intern while in college. Because I didn't, I felt as though I missed out on certain things. I really think that it depends on the internship that you work. Some internships are called internships and it's name only. You're going to get experience but it's very general experience that may not be very beneficial. I think the biggest positive about interning is that it provides an in road for you. You begin to develop a background for yourself and your name becomes known within the company. Internships are valuable tools if they are the right kind of an internship. Some of them are real world experience, but you have to be very selective in the kind of internship that you pursue."

3.   How should the soon-to-be graduate interview?

"I think the sooner you start the better and a big reason for that is that you'll be nervous when you first begin to interview. Employers will look for people who are very comfortable with themselves. They're not looking for a cocky person, but rather a person who has confidence in themselves. Confidence is a big part of it. If you don't have the confidence in yourself then there's no real foundation that will allow you to learn the important things that you'll need to learn for a career.

Basically, if you begin early enough you will get practice with interviewing. Also, because you don't always know what the employer will ask in the interview, you should have an idea of what you want to say and the points that you want to get across. Some employers will ask questions that fit the answers that you want to stress and others will ask questions that really don't allow you to get out the information that you would like. At the end of the interview, most employers will give you the opportunity to summarize your qualifications and I would urge you to take the opportunity to nail home some points that perhaps you may not have been able to express during the actual interview."

4. <u>How can a soon-to-be graduate actually compete against and get hired over more experienced and more qualified candidates</u>?

    "One of the main qualities that we really look for is the desire and drive of a candidate. I don't think anyone will have the desire to land a particular job unless it is something that they're very interested in. So you need to express the interest that you do have. It's not the only criteria that we look for. However, if it's between a candidate who is highly qualified but won't stick with it due to lack of interest versus a candidate that is less qualified but shows a desire to really work in the position I would hire the person with the desire. The reason is they will have the tendency to stick it out, learn the skills that are necessary, and work at becoming successful."

5. <u>What advice would you give the soon-to-be graduate about to enter the Real World</u>?

    "I would advise anyone entering the job market not to settle for any job that you don't truly desire. You'll have a number of interviews and many great opportunities. But you need to select a position you'll enjoy. If you choose a position where your strengths will match the companies strengths then both you and the employer will benefit."

RANDALL D. REGINELLI
Purchasing Director
84 LUMBER COMPANY

1. <u>What do you look for in candidates</u>?

    "The background is the main thing. Where you came from as

far as college experience, extra curricular activities, and are you employed right now. Also, I want to know what you're looking for in a position."

2.   How important are internships?

"Internships are really valuable to the student, especially if you intern in the field that you want to be working in after graduation. Instead of working in a pizza shop or working down at the beach, work a position that will give you some background of the field that you're going to get into. I highly urge students to intern in the field that they want to get into."

3.   How should the soon-to-be-graduate interview?

"You have to come across as really aggressive. And when you go into interview with an employer you should know everything you can about that company. Go to the library and try to research the company. And also about the industry such as where the industry is at and where it's going. If you're looking for a position in retail with my company, 84 Lumber, you should know something about the lumber and home center industry before you come in. That way you can impress me.

Another thing, if you haven't had a job yet, you have to be very aggressive about pursuing the position. You have to tell the employer what you've done in the past. If, for example, you've graduated in May and now it's August and you still don't have a job, you have to express to the employer that over the past four or five months you've been strongly looking for a position. You also have to state things that you have done within that time that kept your mind always working. Whether you stayed up on current events by reading certain magazines or doing math just to keep sharp. But you have to express that if you haven't found a job over the past few months because you could've done nothing. You don't want the employer to think that you've been just wasting away."

4.   How can a soon-to-be-graduate actually compete against and get hired over more experienced and more qualified candidates?

"Basically what you need to show is, although you may not be experienced in that position, you've worked hard throughout college toward obtaining your degree. In the summers, you've interned in your field. You've made good grades. Basically, show that you were successful in the past. All of this will show that you're aggressive and have a strong educational background. You must really push these two points; the aggressiveness to work and a quality educational background."

5.   What advice would you give to the soon-to-be graduate about to enter the Real World?

"The best advice would be to work hard. That's the key. When you come out of school don't look for that $40,000 or $50,000 job right away. Experience is the big thing right now in the job market and you have to take your lumps when starting out. Unless you're in a skilled position, such as a doctor or a lawyer, don't expect to land the $40,000 or $50,000 job right away.

Once you get into a position, you have to give it all you've got and work hard at that position. Always show that you can do better and don't be afraid to work. Many recent graduates get out of school, get the $15,000 to $20,000 job, and they become real depressed about it because they feel they deserve better since they have a college education. Then they usually work the basic nine to five and nothing more. You have to put in your extra time if you're going to make it. When you start off being young, you have to be able to prove yourself. That's the key, working hard and making the most out of the opportunity when you get it."

TIM RODRIGUEZ
Assistant Manager
WALMART

1.   <u>What do you look for in candidates</u>?

"The first thing is appearance. I expect a candidate to look professional regardless of the position they're applying for. Although appearance holds little weight in the overall selection it does tend to create the overall atmosphere for the interview.

The second thing is initiative. People who are self motivated can set themselves far above the other candidates. The candidates who take initiative are the goal setters. They seek the answers to problem situations and they don't passively wait for success. These candidates will usually move up the corporate ladder in an extremely fast pace and these are the kind of people that I want working for my company.

The third thing is responsibility. A candidate applying for any position needs to show that they can handle responsibility. Some examples would be participation in student government, community involvement, captain of an athletic team, or a club representative. Those candidates who can handle responsibility often crave responsibility. These are the go-getters who settle for nothing but the best. People who don't feel comfortable with responsibility will not progress in the future with our company.

The fourth thing is communication. A candidate should be able to express themself openly. For our business, retail, eighty percent of the business is people oriented. Outgoing people who can rate well with the public have a great advantage in our business. I basically spend approximately fifteen percent of my time merchandising, five percent on operations and eighty percent of the time taking care of customers and the associates of Walmart. So it's very

115

important that the candidates I interview be people oriented."

2.   How important are internships?

"The key advantage of participating in an internship is that the student receives real world experience with a major corporation. Also, there are many different summer jobs that students may not realize that require similar initiative, hard work and responsibility on their part. I consider internships and summer jobs to be very important in that it provides practical experience."

3.   How should the soon-to-be-graduate interview?

"The first thing that I look for when interviewing is if the candidate is prepared to expand and be in depth on answers to questions. I ask all open ended questions because I want to get to know the candidate on both a business and personal level. They need to be able to correlate their strengths and skills with the position they're applying for. I don't ask yes or no type questions so candidates need to be able to expand and be prepared to ask questions on their own. I feel my best interviews are those interviews where I feel as though I'm being interviewed by the candidate while at the same time getting to know them."

4.   How can the soon-to-be graduate actually compete against and get hired over more experienced and more qualified candidates?

"You can't hold back when you're in the interview. Don't be afraid to toot your own horn, so to speak. Have confidence in the skills you've acquired in your past experiences. You need to show examples of leadership, initiative and responsibility. You need to be able to match your strengths to what each company is actually looking for in a candidate for that position. One of the most useful ways to prepare for an interview is by using basic business literature to learn the

116

information about the company. It's very beneficial to know this information and will allow you to ask more in depth questions during the interview."

5. <u>What advice would you give the soon-to-be graduate about to enter the Real World</u>?

"There are three basic characteristics that I feel are vital and will give you that competitive edge when you're pursuing a job. The first is perseverance. Those people who are willing to put in the extra time that it's going to take and not thinking twice about it.

The second characteristic is initiative. People who are going to take the initiative are those who strive for the top. I want the person who is going to move up the corporate ladder the fastest. These aren't the people who sit and wait to be told what to do. They're the one's who go out and seek their own opportunities. Sure there will be times when they're going to make mistakes but they will learn from them and better themselves.

The third characteristic that you need is responsibility. You need to be able to handle responsibility and relate to other people. Be able to delegate authority and establish relationships with other people. Be able to take on major tasks and be organized during those tasks. Basically, be able to develop a total organizational plan just through the ability to handle responsibility. So within the past jobs that you've held or college activities be able to show how you've handled responsibility. Make sure that you make those examples known during the interview."

STEPHEN J. BLASCO III
Client Service Specialist
NORRELL SERVICES, INC.

1.   <u>What do you look for in candidates</u>?

"I look for the following characteristics:

* *Good Communication skills*
* *Outgoing to an extent*
* *Easy to talk to and can carry on a conversation*
* *The candidate must be enthusiastic about interviewing*
* *Work history*
* *Someone who is eager for an interview and looks at the situation as an opportunity*
* *Someone who is flexible with places, times, and positions*

Basically, I'm looking for a people person."

2.   <u>How important are internships</u>?

"In this day and age, internships are becoming more important because many companies are downsizing. Many experienced candidates are now forced to re-enter the job market and companies now have a bigger pool of candidates to choose from. Any kind of experience you can gain is very helpful. What we look for is what exactly did you do in the internship? An internship is not mandatory, but is helpful in beating out the competition."

3.   <u>How should the soon-to-be graduate interview</u>?

"I would suggest the candidate be prepared before the interview. Here are a few tips to help you prepare:

* *<u>Question</u>: <u>Tell me about yourself</u>*

Have a 2-3 minute script on yourself prepared that touches

118

on certain areas not mentioned on the resume. Give the interviewer something more than what they are reading on the resume.

* If the interviewer asks for a weakness, turn what may be a negative response into a positive answer. For example, 'My weakness is working with people who procrastinate because I like to get things done in a timely manner.' This shows that the person has high energy and a sense of urgency.

* Keep good eye contact.

* At the end of the interview ask the employer for the next step. You want to know what the process is to get hired. And, if possible, set up that next step immediately with the employer.

* Have success stories of what you've accomplished. Be prepared to answer questions on how you've overcome certain objections in past jobs or life experiences."

4.   <u>How can a soon-to-be graduate actually compete against and get hired over more experienced and more qualified candidates</u>?

"I believe it's all in how you interview. How much research is done on the company is very important. A few suggestions may be:

*   Call people in the industry and get an idea of exactly what they do
*   Look at annual reports to find out where the company is going and how you can be part of it
*   Have a broad background and don't be narrow minded

Basically, you want to do a lot of research on the company

to show the employer that you are very interested in working for them."

5. <u>What advice would you give the soon-to-be graduate about to enter the Real World</u>?

"Talk to as many people as possible to get your name circulating. Let it be known that you are looking for a job and visit job fairs. Pick the areas that you would like to work and visit the companies in person to drop off your resume.

Also, you may want to register with temporary help services or employment agencies. These services have general positions as well as positions in the areas of technical, accounting, law, etc... Many companies are using these services rather than placing adds and getting flooded with resumes. In addition, these services can provide a graduate with experience that they may not have."

AMY GORDON
Store Manager / District Recruiter
STRUCTURE (Division of The Limited Corp.)

1. <u>What do you look for in candidates</u>?

"One of the things that we look at is your background experience. Since we are in the retail business, we look to see if you've ever worked in the retail industry. It's not necessarily required but it's more favorable if you have because you understand what our job is all about.

We do look to see if you've graduated from college and, if so, what type of degree you hold. If you have an engineering degree and you're now trying to enter the retail industry, we tend to question why you are changing fields.

We look at any activities you participated in while attending

120

college. Did you hold any type of position, did you have any responsibilities, did you show any leadership in an activity that you've done?"

2. How important are internships?

    "Obviously if you have interned it will benefit you. It shows that you have a better understanding of what the job is all about. If someone is interested in retail then while you're in school you should try to work part time in the industry. Maybe you're only working part time and you're not actually interning, but at least your learning about the industry."

3. How should the soon-to-be graduate interview?

    "You have to realize that just because you graduate from college, it doesn't automatically make you more qualified for a higher position. I interview a lot of people who think that since they have a college degree they should start at a higher position than what they're actually qualified for.

    In our company there are three levels: assistant manager, co-manager, store manager. One thing that we always find when we interview students right out of college is that they automatically think they should be a co-manager. Students don't realize that they haven't had any management or retail experience and they need to understand that in order to work your way up through a company you need to start at the bottom. Starting at the bottom is not always a bad thing. Students come out of college thinking that they're going to make a certain amount of money just because they have a degree. It doesn't work that way.

    Personally, I want a candidate that is right out of college who I'm interviewing to basically tell me that they don't mind starting at the bottom so they can learn everything that they can possibly learn. That says more to me than a candidate who tells me they're qualified to be a co-manager because they have a college degree. You need to be confident, but not overly confident. You need to understand what the job is all about. You need to understand what the retail business is and what it takes to be a manager in the retail business. You should also learn the background of the company that you are interviewing with. This shows me that you really want to work for my company."

4.   How can a soon-to-be graduate actually compete against and get hired over more experienced and more qualified candidates?

"I think your confidence level is very important. We interview many people who have a lot of experience but sometimes hiring a candidate with a lot of experience isn't always the best choice. Some candidates are set in their ways and are not able to change how they think about things. I would look at someone new and fresh as someone that we can mold and teach our way while not having to worry about overcoming their old patterns. That's something that you may want to stress to the employer during your interview."

5.   What advice would you give the soon-to-be graduate about to enter the Real World?

"Don't expect a higher position because you have a degree. You have to understand that going to college was a stepping stone. It's simply a learning experience, a notch on your belt. It doesn't automatically qualify you for a position. A degree is a great accomplishment and you've worked hard for it. But in reality you have to start all over again just as you begin college as a freshman. Now you're starting in a job and sometimes you have to start at the bottom. It's real important for you to understand that."

Let's Join Together in the Fight Against Cancer!

Dear Friend:

Since my sister Vicki's death from cancer in 1991, I have been searching for a way to fight back against this terrible disease. I have found a way for all of us to join together to eliminate this evil disease from our lives. Please help!

-James Malinchak

The V Foundation is a charitable organization dedicated to saving lives by helping to find a cure for cancer. It seeks to create an urgent awareness among all Americans of the importance of the fight against cancer and to generate broad-based support for cancer research. The foundation performs these dual roles through advocacy, education, fund raising and philanthropy. The V Foundation carries on Jim Valvano's name and empowers others with his winning spirit, carrying on the creed he lived by:

"Don't Give Up, Don't Ever Give Up!"

Jim Valvano, with the support of ESPN, created **The V Foundation,** a non-profit, tax-exempt foundation that seeks to raise funds to further cancer research and promote awareness of the disease. The former NC State basketball coach, who died of cancer at the age of 47 in April 1993, was awarded the inaugural *Arthur Ashe Award for Courage* at The ESPYs, hosted by ESPN. In his acceptance speech, Coach V pleaded: *"...one in every four will be afflicted with this disease, and yet somehow, we seem to have put it in a little bit of the background. I want to bring it back on the front table. We need your help. We need money for research. It may not save my life. It may not save my children's lives. It may save someone you love...we are starting the **Jimmy V Foundation for Cancer Research** and its motto is: "Don't Give Up, Don't Ever Give Up!"*

If you would like to make a contribution or learn more information, contact:

The V Foundation
1201 Walnut Street, 2nd Floor
Cary, NC 27511
1-800-4-JIMMY V
www.jimmyv.org

123

"YOU CAN DO IT!"

"America's Hottest Young Speaker"

Recognized by promoters worldwide as one of the most outstanding young speakers, James captivates and involves his audiences with his blend of energy, enthusiasm, knowledge and humor.

To invite James Malinchak to speak at your school or conference, contact:

James Malinchak International
P.O. Box 3944
Beverly Hills, CA 90212-0944
(954) 796-1925 or Email: JamesMal@aol.com

** Special Bonus **
Schedule James and receive 100 FREE BOOKS

Rave Reviews from Colleges

"Fantastic! Phenomenal! One of the most helpful speakers we've ever had."
-Clayton Kua, Director of Alumni Affairs, Univ. of Hawaii at Hilo

"Excellent presentation! All the students recommended we invite you back."
-Suzanne Ashe, Events Coordinator, Cerritos (CA) Community College

"Unbelievable! James was fantastic to work with. All the Student Organization leaders attending thought the presentations were the *best* they have ever attended!"
-Dana Marolt, Student Government Chair, Hope College (Holland, MI)

"James was an outstanding lecturer and his program was very beneficial to the students. I would recommend him to any college or university!"
-Steven Talbot, Stud. Prgmmg. Assc., Nicholls State Univ. (Thibodaux, LA)

"Your presentation, *From College to the Real World,* was incredible! The success of our Career Day was due, in large part, to your motivating presence."
-Jan Swinton, Coord. of Projects, Glendale (CA) Community College

"Great talk on a great book! You need to get the word out to as many students as possible. It is important information they rarely get from their professors."
-William Wilson, Professor, George Washington Univ. (Washington, DC)

Rave Reviews from Top Speakers

"James Malinchak's strategies have the power to change lives!"
-Jack Canfield, Co-author
#1 New York Times Bestseller, *Chicken Soup for the Soul*

"James Malinchak has an unlimited future as a speaker serving his audiences brilliant insights with great love!"
-Mark Victor Hansen, Co-author
#1 New York Times Bestseller, *Chicken Soup for the Soul*

"James Malinchak speaks with enthusiasm, great content and passion to help you push to another level!"
-Peter Legge, named by *Toastmasters International* **as one of the**
Top 5 Speakers in North America

James Malinchak's Self-Improvement and Success Books
(Great Gift Ideas!)

Name:_____

Address:_____

City/State/Zip:_____

Telephone:_____ Email:_____

_____ copies *From College to the Real World* $ 11.95 _____

_____ copies *Teenagers Tips for Success* $ 9.95 _____

_____ copies *The Master Networker* $ 3.00 _____

_____ copies *The Expert Writer* $ 3.00 _____

No shipping charge for books mailed to US or Canada.

Tax on books shipped to California addresses is 8%   _____

No Telephone Orders   Total: $ _____

Discounts available for multiple copies. Call for details (954) 796-1925

Please send a check or money order for the total amount payable to:

Positive Publishing - c/o P.O. Box 3944 - Beverly Hills, CA 90212-0944